CHINESE
COOKERY
VEGETARIAN
DELICACIES

CHINESE COOKERY
VEGETARIAN DELICACIES

Sangeeta Khanna

STERLING PUBLISHERS PRIVATE LIMITED

STERLING PUBLISHERS PRIVATE LIMITED
L-10, Green Park Extension, New Delhi - 110 016

Chinese Cookery: Vegetarian Delicacies
© 1989, Sangeeta Khanna
Reprint 1992, 1995, 1996

Cover : Vegetable noodles garnished with wanton fried, chilli, garlic sauce and chillies in vinegar

PRINTED IN INDIA

Published by S.K. Ghai, Managing Director, Sterling Publishers Pvt. Ltd., L-10, Green Park Extension, New Delhi-110 016. Photocomposed at Scanset, New Delhi.
Printed at Baba Barkhanath, New Delhi.

Dedicated to my Grandparents Late Smt. CHANAN DEVI KAPOOR and late Shri RAMLAL KAPOOR and my father-in-law late Shri SARB PRAKASH KHANNA and my father late Shri TILAK RAJ KAPOOR.

COLOURED PLATES

CONTENTS

INTRODUCTION

I present in this book most of my Vegetarian Chinese recipes highly appreciated by my students all over India and those visiting from other countries such as Singapore, Hong Kong, Gulf countries, USA, Canada and France who come and attend my classes. All recipes are kept simple. Every step in the making of a particular dish is explained in detail, keeping back none of the secrets. Most of the recipes in this book are economical and quick and should not take more than 15 minutes of preparation time.

I have arranged the recipes in four topics, viz., Soups & Salads, Main Dishes, Baked Dishes, Party Snacks & Puddings. Since rice and noodles are the staple of Chinese food, use has been made of them in about 40 per cent of the recipes. Soup is not necessarily the first course in a Chinese meal, but the soups have been presented in the first chapter. Soya bean sauce, garlic and vinegar are often used in small quantities in groups for extra flavour. Since desserts are not essentially a part of a Chinese meal, you will find very few in this book but all the desserts given in this book are doubly tested and if you like, you could finish a meal this way.

The main cooking equipment is a wok. It is a bowl shaped large iron vessel, as wide as an Indian Karahi. The principal cooking medium is any refined oil, preferably peanut oil. The best aid to eating is forks and spoons if one is not used to eating with chopsticks.

In Chinese cooking, milk and milk products are almost completely absent. However, I have at some places made use of milk to make the batter, instead of eggs which is normally used, catering mainly for the strict vegetarians. Also Bean Curd which is considered a vegetable in Chinese food, is not easily available in India, so Paneer made out of milk can be substituted for Bean Curd. But wherever Bean Curd is procurable, its use should be made of as it has a very high protein content and is very nutritious. Soft Bean Curd is used for salads and firmer kind is used for dishes as a vegetable.

Deep frying, stir frying and braising are the methods mainly used in Chinese cooking. Cutting of the vegetables is most important in the preparation of Chinese food and I have tried to explain the way of cutting with the help of self drawn sketches to make things easier for a novice. Special attention has been paid in selecting the easily procurable vegetables in most of the dishes, keeping also in mind their nutrient value. Flavouring such as with garlic and ginger have often been used in the recipes. However, green chilli paste, chilli sauce, capsico sauce could be deleted for the discerning Western users. The vegetables for the Chinese cooking could be cut well in advance and kept in the fridge compartment individually packed in polythene bags and closed with rubber bands.

Most of the recipes presented in this book can be successfully adapted and variated into non-vegetarian dishes.

I do hope this book will make interesting reading and will be an exciting experience while trying your hand at a recipe and will shape you into an excellent cook.

Cutting of Vegetables for Chinese Cooking

Chopping and slicing are two ways of cutting vegetables for Chinese cooking. Given on page 15 are sketches showing the chopping and slicing of various vegetables.

Sketch (a)	:	Cutting of Carrot and Celery diagonally into thin slices.
Sketch (b)	:	Celery.
Sketch (c) & (d)	:	Cutting of Capsicum in two different ways.
Sketch (e)	:	Chopping of Spring Onion.
Sketch (f)	:	Slicing of Onion.

Weights & Measures

The weights and measures used in this book are the standard weighing cups and grammes. One cup measures approximately 200 gms and 1 tsp which is meant to represent 1 level teaspoon is equivalent to approximately 5 grammes. Similarly 1 tbsp measuring 1 level tablespoon is equivalent to approximately 15 grammes or 3 teaspoons.

Oven temperature mostly used in baked dishes is 200⁰ Centigrade which is equivalent to approximately 400⁰ Fahrenheit or Gas mark 6.

GLOSSARY

Some of the commonly used ingredients and items used in Chinese cooking are listed below:

Bamboo Shoots

Not easily available in India as fresh bamboo shoots. There may be difficulty in procuring fresh bamboo shoots but canned are freely available in large departmental stores.

Bean Curd

It looks like soft cheese, white in colour. It is made out of boiled soya bean milk and is cut into cubical pieces of about one inch size. Since it is not at all procurable in India, "Paneer" made out of milk will have to be made use of instead of bean curd for the recipes given in this book (though paneer is not used in Chinese cooking). Bean curd has a high vegetable protein content and is very nutritious. One could hunt for this item in bigger departmental stores, where it should be available in polythene packs. To use, it has to be soaked in warm water for 15 minutes adding 1/2 tsp baking soda for 250 grammes bean curd, then to be rinsed in cold water 2-3 times.

Bean Sprout

There are two kinds of bean sprout — one made out of soya bean and the other out of green gram (whole moong). Green gram or moong beans are easily available in India and can be grown indoors. Moong beans are extensively used in India and a common ingredient for most Chinese main dishes.

To prepare bean sprout, take half cup of washed green gram and take one cup water to cover green gram. Soak for 12 hours. Drain water and tie in a damp cloth. Put it in a warm place for 4 to 5 days. (Rinse with fresh water everyday.) The sprouts will be ready in 4 to 5 days. Seal them in polythene packs to retain freshness and put in fridge. Use as required.

Ready-to-use bean sprouts are also available in large departmental stores.

Broccoli
It is a green looking vegetable used in Chinese main and side dishes. If not available, cauliflower can be substituted.

Celery
Green leafy vegetable available with stalk and root used mostly for soups and braised dishes.

Dried Mushrooms
Used extensively in Chinese cooking. Available in polythene in departmental stores. To use dried mushrooms, soak in warm water for half an hour. Drain off water and use as directed in the recipe. Dried mushrooms are richer in flavour compared to fresh mushrooms. If not available fresh mushrooms can be substituted.

Monosodium Glutamate (Ajinomoto)
Also called Chinese tasting salt. Should be used in little quantities, in this book, not more than half tsp for any recipe. It brings out the natural flavours in food, but is entirely optional for usage.

Rice Noodles
Rice noodles are made out of rice flour. Ready-to-use rice noodles are available in large departmental stores, in polythene packs. These should not be boiled like normal noodles but should be soaked in lukewarm water for 15 minutes. Drain water before using.

Spring Onion
Also called Scallion. It is extensively used in Chinese cooking. Only the green stalk is used, discarding the onion part. Green stalk is chopped fine and used as directed in the recipes.

Szechuan Pepper
Mostly used in braised Chinese dishes. It is highly aromatic and therefore gives strong flavour.

Star Anise
Star shaped spice, brown in colour and is used only for flavouring dishes. It is removed from the dish before serving.

Five-spice powder
Made out of a mixture of star anise, szechuan pepper, cloves, cinnamon and fennell. These five spices are ground together in small quantities. The five-spice powder itself is used in very small quantities, mostly in braised dishes.

Sesame Seed Oil

Ready to use sesame seed oil is available in departmental stores. It is a strongly flavoured seasoning oil, prepared from sesame seeds.

Soya Bean Sauce

Made out of soya bean seeds. Extensively used in Chinese cooking and also as table ingredient because of its saltiness. Ready-to-use soya bean sauce available in different packings in all departmental stores.

Worcestershire Sauce

Made out of brewed vinegar, cane sugar, acetic acid, tamarind juice, jaggery, salt, spices, condiment and malt extract. Used for snacks and soups for enriched flavour and taste.

8 to 8 Sauce

Made out of jaggery, dates, tamarind and liquid spices extracts. It is excellent for enriching the flavour of dishes and adds taste to soups, salads and dishes. Available in large departmental stores.

Cocktail Sauce

Ready-to-use Cocktail sauce available in departmental stores. It is served with Chinese snacks. To prepare at home, take 1/2 cup chilli sauce, juice of 1 lime, 6 drops of tomato sauce, 1 tsp of 8 to 8 sauce, 1 tsp of worcestershire sauce. Combine them and add salt to taste.

OTHER COMMON INGREDIENTS

The above are basic ingredients used in Chinese cooking. Apart from these, the other ingredients repeatedly used in this book and their methods of preparation are :

Green Chilli Sauce

Ready-to-use green chilli sauce is readily available in departmental stores. However, if one were to prepare fresh chilli sauce, the method is as follows:

Take the following ingredients :

10 fresh green chillies, 1/2 inch piece ginger, 6 cloves garlic, 2 minced shallots, 1 tbsp water, 1 tsp soya bean sauce, 2 tsp tomato sauce, 2 tablespoons vinegar, 1 tbsp sugar (or sugar to taste) and salt to taste.

Mix above ingredients and grind in a mixie and serve as required.

Red Chilli Sauce

This is also available in departmental stores in bottle packings. For preparing it fresh, take the following :

6 dry red chillies, 3 teaspoon sugar, 6 cloves garlic, juice of one lime, 3 tsp vinegar, 3 tbsp tomato sauce and salt to taste.

Mix these ingredients in a mixie and serve as required.

Vegetable Stock

Various soups and some other dishes given in this book have used vegetable stock. The method is given below, instead of repeating in all recipes. This will make 5 cups of vegetable stock.

Ingredients: 1 cup mixed sliced vegetables (cabbage, carrot, beans, cauliflower), 6 cups water, 1 small sliced onion, 1/2 chopped stalk celery, 1 tsp ginger paste, 1/2 tsp salt.

Method
1. Mix the vegetables, celery, ginger paste, onion, salt and 6 cups water and boil in a pressure cooker for 5 minutes after first whistle.
2. Remove from fire and cool.
3. Strain stock and use as directed.

Ginger Paste

Almost all dishes use ginger and garlic pastes. For making ginger paste, wash ginger and peel off the outer skin with a knife or a peeler. Slice about 1 inch ginger piece and pound well. This will make about 1 tsp paste. With experience one would know how much ginger to pound for getting the right quantity of paste.

Garlic Paste

Similarly garlic paste is made by pounding garlic cloves. Take 12 medium sized garlic cloves and peel off the outer skin with a knife. Pound well to get about 1 tsp paste.

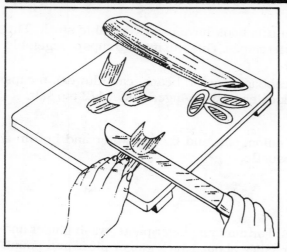
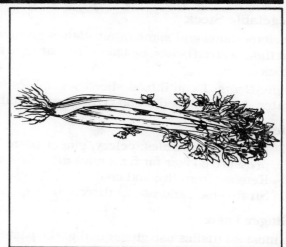
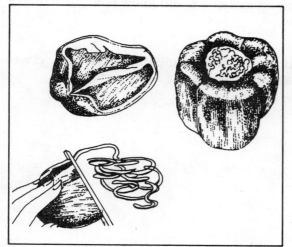
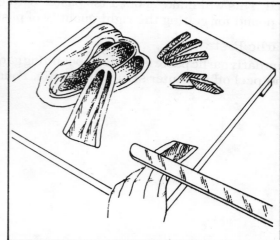
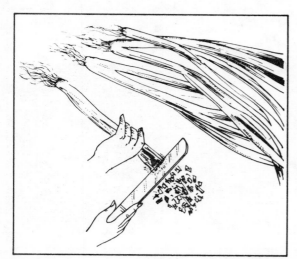
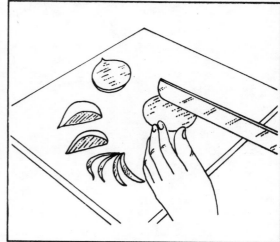

Cutting and Slicing of Chinese Vegetables

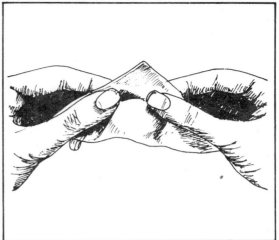
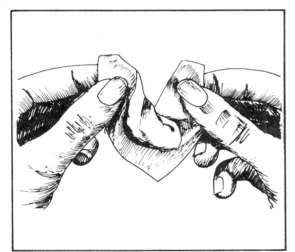
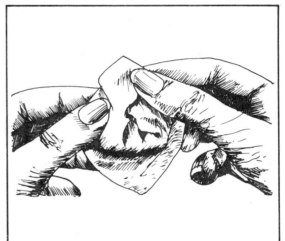
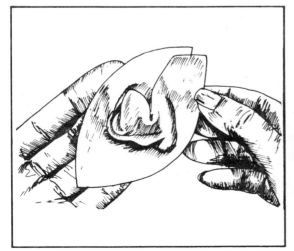

Different Steps in Making of Wontons

Different Steps in Making of Carbon

SOUPS AND SALADS

VEGETABLE CORN SOUP
Serves - 5

INGREDIENTS

1	cup mixed vegetables (carrot, beans, cauliflower, peas)
1/2	cup capsicum cut into small bits
1/2	cup chopped spring onion
1	tin sweet corn cream
5	tbsp cornflour
1	tsp white pepper
1/2	tsp ajinomoto
8	cups water
	salt to taste

METHOD

1. Boil 1 cup mixed vegetables and 8 cups water in a pressure cooker for 5 minutes after the whistle.
2. Strain it and take the stock, mix the stock with sweet corn cream and boil together for 5 minutes.
3. Add salt, white pepper and ajinomoto.
4. Dissolve cornflour in half cup boiled and cooled water and add to the above soup, stirring continuously.
5. Cook for about 2 minutes, till it reaches the required thickness of the soup.
6. Add chopped capsicum and spring onion and remove from fire.
7. Serve hot.

Note: Also, beaten egg white of 2 eggs could be added into the boiling soup through a strainer.

CREAM OF MUSHROOM SOUP

Serves - 4

INGREDIENTS

1	cup mixed vegetables (cauliflower, carrot, beans and peas)	1	tbsp cornflour
		1	tbsp butter
6	cups water	1/2	tsp ajinomoto
2	tbsp Chinese mushrooms		salt to taste
			white pepper to taste

METHOD

1. Boil the mixed vegetables in 5 cups water for 10 minutes. Strain and take the vegetable stock. Cool it.
2. Boil mushrooms in 1 cup water for 10 minutes. Drain the water and chop the mushrooms.
3. Heat butter in a heavy bottom pan. Add cornflour and roast the cornflour to light brown. Add the cooled vegetable stock.
4. Season well with salt and white pepper.
5. Add chopped mushroom and ajinomoto.
6. Serve hot with soya bean sauce and vinegar.

BEAN SPROUT & BAMBOO SHOOT SOUP
Serves - 4

INGREDIENTS

1/2	cup bean sprout	1	tsp soya bean sauce
1/2	cup chopped bamboo shoots	1	tbsp oil
1/4	cup chopped spring onion	1	tsp white pepper
2	tbsp cornflour	1/8	tsp ajinomoto
5	cups vegetable stock or water		salt to taste

METHOD

1. Heat oil in a wok and saute chopped bamboo shoots and bean sprout for a minute.
2. Add vegetable stock or water with soya bean sauce, ajinomoto, white pepper, spring onion and salt.
3. Mix well and simmer for 5 minutes.
4. Dissolve cornflour in 1/2 cup of boiled and cooled water and add to the above soup.
5. Simmer for another 5 minutes till soup is thick.
6. Serve hot with chilli sauce and vinegar.

CABBAGE SOUP WITH CELERY
Serves - 4

INGREDIENTS

1	cup chopped cabbage		2	tbsp cornflour
2	chopped celery stalks (without leaves)		1/2	cup water for cornflour
1/2	cup chopped spring onion		1	tsp soyabean sauce
6	cups water or vegetable stock		1	tsp oil
1/4	tsp ginger paste			salt to taste
1/4	tsp garlic paste			white pepper to taste

METHOD

1. Heat oil in a wok. Fry ginger and garlic paste. Add chopped spring onion. Saute for a second and add vegetable stock.
2. Cook for 10 minutes, adding chopped cabbage, chopped celery stalk, soya bean sauce, salt and pepper to taste.
3. Dissolve cornflour in water and add to the boiling soup. Cook till the soup thickens.
4. Serve hot with chilli sauce.

HOT AND SOUR SOUP
Serves - 4

INGREDIENTS

1	cup mixed chopped vegetables (cabbage, carrot, beans and cauliflower)	6	cups water
		1	green chilli
1	cup chopped spring onion	2	tsp lime juice
1	finely shredded carrot	1	tbsp chopped parsley leaves
1	tbsp cornflour	1/2	tsp oil
1/2	tsp ginger paste	1/2	tsp white pepper
1/4	tsp garlic paste		salt to taste

METHOD

1. Take 1 cup chopped mixed vegetables and add 6 cups water to it.
2. Boil in the pressure cooker for 5 minutes after the first whistle.
3. Remove from the fire. Open the pressure cooker lid, strain the water and take the stock.
4. Heat the oil and fry ginger and garlic paste to light brown. Pour the vegetable stock in it and let both boil for 5 minutes.
5. Add carrot shreds, green chilli paste, parsley leaves, salt and white pepper and cook for another 2 minutes.
6. Dissolve cornflour in a quarter cup water and add to the above soup.
7. Take off fire, add lime juice and spring onion stalk.
8. Serve hot.

WONTON SOUP
Serves-5

INGREDIENTS

For wonton :
1/2 cup flour, 2 tbsp cornflour
1/2 egg, 3-4 tbsp water to knead dough, pinch of salt

For wonton filling
1   tbsp chopped capsicum
1/4 tsp ajinomoto
1   tbsp finely chopped bamboo shoot
1/2 tsp sugar
1   tbsp spring onion stalk

1   tbsp oil
1   tbsp grated carrot
     salt to taste
1   flake garlic
     pepper to taste
1   tsp chopped coriander leaves

For the soup
6   cups vegetable stock
2   chopped spring onion
1/2 thinly sliced cucumber

METHOD

1. Beat the egg with water and add the flour and cornflour.
2. Stir thoroughly until well mixed. Knead for about 5 minutes into a stiff dough.
3. Cover the dough with a damp cloth and leave it aside for 1/2 hour.
4. Roll out thin and cut into small squares (about 2 inches) and make 15 wonton skin.
5. Mix spring onion stalk, carrot, capsicum and bamboo shoot.
6. Heat oil in a wok. Saute garlic, then add mixed vegetables along with chopped coriander leaves, sugar, salt, pepper and ajinomoto.
7. Stir fry the above filling for a minute. Remove from fire and cool it.
8. Put little filling in the centre of each skin. Dampen one side with water and fold as shown on page 16.
9. Cook wonton in salted water for 15 minutes on medium flame. Then drain.
10. Bring the vegetable stock to boiling and add cooked wonton, spring onion, ajino-moto and sliced cucumber.
11. Serve hot.

Note: If not using egg, make wonton dough with chilled water (quantity as required to form a smooth dough).

TOMATO AND EGG DROP SOUP

Serves - 4

INGREDIENTS

4	tomatoes		1	tsp soya bean sauce
8	cups water		3	tbsp oil
2	eggs		1	tbsp parsley
1	sliced onion		1	star anise
1/4	tsp garlic paste			pinch of ajinomoto
1/4	tsp ginger paste			salt to taste
1	tbsp cornflour			pepper to taste

METHOD

1. To remove the skin of tomatoes, put them in boiling water and immediately shift them to cold water.
2. Peel the skin and cut them into small bits or cubes.
3. Heat oil in a wok. Fry ginger and garlic pastes for a second. Add sliced onion and cook till onion is transparent.
4. Add tomatoes to it and cook together for 2 minutes.
5. Dissolve cornflour in 8 cups water and add to above mixture.
6. Add salt and pepper to taste. Add chopped parsley leaves and soya bean sauce along with ajinomoto and star anise.
7. Cook the soup till it starts boiling thoroughly.
8. Beat eggs with a pinch of salt and sieve it through the strainer into the boiling soup, stirring continuously.
9. Serve immediately in soup bowls. Remove star anise before serving.

NOODLE SOUP
Serves - 3

INGREDIENTS

100	gms noodles		1	tsp oil
6	cups vegetable stock		1	tbsp soya bean sauce
1/2	cup chopped spring onion		1/2	tsp pepper
1/2	tsp garlic paste			pinch of ajinomoto
1/2	tsp ginger paste		1	tsp sherry
1	tbsp cornflour			salt to taste

METHOD

1. Heat oil in a wok. Add ginger and garlic paste to it. Fry for a minute. Then add vegetable stock, cook for 5 minutes, adding salt, pepper and ajinomoto.
2. Soak cornflour in 2 tablespoons water and add to the above soup.
3. Add soya bean sauce and sherry.
4. Boil noodles in salted water. Drain and place them in individual bowls.
5. Pour the prepared stock on noodles. Top with chopped spring onion.
6. Serve with chilli sauce.

TOMATO SOUP WITH SPINACH PUREE

Serves -4

INGREDIENTS

1	kg tomatoes		1/2	cup water for cornflour
8	cups water		1	tsp soya bean sauce
1/2	kg spinach		1/8+1/8	tsp ajinomoto
1/2	tsp crushed garlic		1/2	tsp pepper
1	potato		salt to taste	
2	tbsp butter			
1-2	tbsp cornflour			

METHOD

1. Boil chopped tomatoes with 6 cups water, garlic and peeled and chopped potato in a pressure cooker for 5 minutes after the first whistle.
2. Cool and grind in a mixie.
3. Strain and keep aside.
4. Wash spinach, take leaves and tender stalk and boil in 2 cup water for 5 minutes. Add 1/8 teaspoon ajinomoto.
5. Cool and grind in a mixie. Add pinch of salt and pepper. Take strained tomato juice in a saucepan, add soya bean sauce, sugar, pepper and butter to it, along with 1/8 teaspoon ajinomoto.
6. Boil for 5 minutes, then add cornflour dissolved in water.
7. Thicken the soup as required, by increasing or reducing the cornflour quantity.
8. Serve the soup hot in a soup bowl with 1 teaspoon spinach puree as topping.

VEGETABLE NOODLE SOUP
Serves - 4

INGREDIENTS

1	cup boiled noodles		1	thinly sliced carrot
6	cups vegetable stock		2	tbsp cornflour
1/4	cup peas		2	tbsp water for cornflour
1	cup chopped spring onion stalk		1/4	tsp ajinomoto
1/4	cup dried mushroom			salt to taste
2	tbsp shredded bamboo shoot			pepper to taste

METHOD

1. Boil noodles in boiling hot water for 2 minutes.
2. Drain, wash under tap water, apply 1 tablespoon oil to the noodles and keep aside.
3. Boil peas in 1/2 cup water and keep aside. Boil mushrooms in water and keep aside.
4. Heat vegetable stock in a heavy bottomed pan or skillet. Add peas, boiled mushrooms, bamboo shoots carrot and spring onion.
5. Cook for 5 minutes.
6. Dissolve cornflour in water and add to above.
7. Add salt, pepper and ajinomoto to it.
8. Add boiled noodles just before serving and bring to boil for one minute.
9. Serve hot with chillies in vinegar and chilli sauce.

SWEET & SOUR SOUP
Serves - 4

INGREDIENTS

6	cups vegetable stock		1/3	cup vinegar
2 1/2	tbsp cornflour		1/3	cup sugar
1/2	cup water for cornflour		1	tsp salt
1	cup chopped spring onion		1/4	tsp ajinomoto
1	cup chopped cucumber			pinch of orange red colour
4-5	boiled wonton			salt to taste
5	tbsp tomato sauce			pepper to taste

METHOD

1. Make vegetable stock and add vinegar, sugar, tomato sauce, salt and pepper to it. Boil for 5 minutes together.
2. Add ajinomoto and orange red colour to it.
3. Dissolve cornflour in water and add to the above mixture, cook for 2 minutes.
4. Add spring onion, cucumber and boiled wonton at the time of reheating and serving.

Note : Make wonton as on page 76 and follow up to step 6.

COLD SALAD CHINESE STYLE

Serves - 5

INGREDIENTS

1	packet lemon jelly
2	cups hot water
1½	cup shredded cabbage
2	chopped capsicums
1	tsp chopped celery
3/4	cup mayonnaise
1	tsp soya bean sauce

1	tsp capsico sauce
2	tbsp sugar
2	pineapple slices
2	tsp vinegar
	white pepper to taste
	salt to taste

METHOD

1. Make jelly by dissolving the jelly powder in 2 cups water. Add 2 tablespoons sugar to it.
2. Set the jelly in freezer till partially set.
3. Beat it with an egg beater or in a mixie till light and fluffy.
4. Add chopped capsicums, shredded cabbage, mayonnaise, chopped celery, vinegar, soya bean sauce, capsico sauce, salt and pepper.
5. Chop the pineapple slices into small pieces and add to the above mixture.
6. Pour it in a greased tin and chill.
7. When fully set, unmould it into a serving dish by putting the tin in hot water for a second.
8. Decorate with lettuce leaves and carrot strips.

CAPSICUM BEAN SPROUT SALAD

Serves - 3

INGREDIENTS

1	sliced capsicum		1	tbsp salad oil
1	cup beans sprout		1	tbsp tamarind pulp
1	cup shredded cabbage		1	tbsp sugar
1	tbsp chopped mint leaves		1/4	tsp ajinomoto
2	slit green chillies			salt to taste
1	cup chopped paneer			white pepper to taste
1	tsp lime juice			

METHOD

1. Mix capsicum, bean sprout, cabbage shreds, mint leaves, green chillies and chopped paneer.
2. Soak tamarind in 2 tablespoons hot water for 10 minutes and strain the juice. Add sugar to it.
3. Mix lime juice, tamarind juice, salt and white pepper and add to cabbage, capsicum mixture.
4. Add salad oil and ajinomoto to it and serve immediately. (If not serving immediately, mix in capsicum, bean sprout and cabbage shreds only at the time of serving. Till such time keep them in chilled water.)

MAIN DISHES

PEAS FRIED RICE
Serves - 3

INGREDIENTS

200	gms rice	1/2	tsp ginger paste
1	tin boiled peas or	2	tbsp soya bean sauce
250	gms shelled peas	4	tbsp oil
2	sliced celery stalks		pinch of ajinomoto
1	sliced onion		salt to taste
1/2	tsp garlic paste		pepper to taste

METHOD

1. Boil rice till tender. Drain off water and dry on a butter paper.
2. Drain off water from tinned peas or shelled fresh peas and boil them in half cup water.
3. Heat oil in a wok. Fry onion. Add ginger and garlic pastes and fry together for a minute.
4. Add peas and celery and fry for another minute.
5. Add rice, flame slow. Mix well, adding salt, pepper, soya bean sauce and ajinomoto and cook for 2 minutes.

MUSHROOM FRIED RICE

Serves - 4

INGREDIENTS

2 1/2 cups (500 gms) rice
200 gms fresh mushrooms
   or
(half cup tinned mushrooms)
1/4 cup bamboo shoots
2 eggs (Optional)
1/2 cup spring onion

1/2 cup refined oil
2 tbsp soya sauce
1/4 tsp white pepper powder
1/4 tsp ajinomoto
4 tbsp vinegar
2 tbsp tomato sauce
salt to taste

METHOD

1. Boil the fresh mushrooms in 1 1/2 cups water for about 10 minutes (if using tinned mushrooms, do not boil).
2. Drain off water, discard the stem and chop the caps into square pieces.
3. Chop the spring onions and bamboo shoots fine.
4. Boil rice in 8 cups water with 1/2 teaspoon salt and 1/2 teaspoon refined oil.
5. Strain, drain off water and spread on a clean paper to dry and cool.
6. Heat quarter cup oil in a pan, add spring onions, mushrooms and bamboo shoots and stir for one minute.
7. Remove from the pan and leave to cool.
8. Heat the remaining oil in the pan, add cooked rice along with fried mushrooms, bamboo shoots and spring onion.
9. Mix in the sauces and vinegar, season with salt, pepper and ajinomoto.
10. Stir continuously till sauces dry. Remove from fire and serve hot.
11. If using eggs, lightly beat them with a little salt, heat one tablespoon oil in a frying pan, add the beaten eggs and cook to make an omelette. Break into pieces or strips and fold into the rice mixture, while mixing the mushrooms, spring onion and bamboo shoots as in (8) above.

FRIED RICE WITH CHILLI GRAVY

Serves - 4

INGREDIENTS

For the fried rice

2	cups boiled rice
2	tbsp oil, salt to taste

For the chilli gravy

2	tbsp chopped green chillies
1	tsp cumin seed
1	tsp soya bean sauce
4	dry red chillies

1	tbsp tomato sauce
1/2	cup chopped tomatoes
1	tbsp vinegar
1	tbsp cornflour
1/2	tsp sugar
1¹/₂	cups water
1	tbsp chopped cashewnuts
1	tbsp oil
	salt to taste
	pepper to taste

METHOD

For the Fried Rice

1. Heat 2 tablespoons oil in a wok.
2. Fry boiled rice in it for a minute. Add salt to taste.
3. Arrange rice in a serving dish.

For the Gravy

1. Boil green chillies in 1¹/₂ cups water for 5 minutes.
2. Drain off water and keep aside.
3. Heat 1 tablespoon oil in a wok. Add cumin seed, red chillies and chopped cashewnuts and fry for a second.
4. Remove from fire, cool and grind it to a paste.
5. Mix this paste with the boiled chopped chillies.
6. Add remaining 1 tablespoon oil and fry chopped tomatoes.
7. Add soya bean sauce, vinegar, tomato sauce, sugar to it and mix   together for a minute.
8. Add ground chilli paste to the above sauce and stir fry for a second.
9. Add salt and pepper to taste.
10. Dissolve cornflour in water and add to the above mixture.
11. Cook till thickened to gravy consistency.
12. Pour this chilli gravy as topping on fried rice or serve it along with fried rice.

VEGETABLE FRIED RICE
Serves - 4

INGREDIENTS

2¹/₂ cups (500 gms) rice
1   bunch spring onion
1/2 cup chopped carrot
1/2 cup chopped capsicum
1/4 cup beans
1/2 cup boiled peas
1/2 tbsp ginger paste
1/2 tbsp garlic paste

1/2 tsp white pepper powder
1/4 tsp ajinomoto
2   tbsp soyabean sauce
4   tbsp vinegar
2   tbsp tomato sauce
1/2 cup refined oil
1   tsp salt (or salt to taste)

METHOD

1. Boil rice in water with half teaspoon salt and half teaspoon refined oil till cooked.
2. Strain to drain out water and spread on a clean paper to dry and cool.
3. Chop the spring onion fine and slice vegetables, i.e. carrot, capsicum and beans fine.
4. Make a paste of ginger and garlic.
5. In wok (Chinese karahi) or a wide frying pan, heat a quarter cup oil, add ginger-garlic paste and when light brown, add beans, carrot, capsicum, green peas and spring onion.
6. Stir-fry briefly and pour into another dish.
7. Wipe the wok dry and add remaining quarter cup oil and heat over full flame until very hot. Add the boiled, dried and cold rice.
8. Stir-fry the rice over low flame for approximately three minutes.
9. Add all the fried vegetables along with spring onion and mix in soya sauce, vinegar, tomato sauce, salt, white pepper and ajinomoto and bring back on full flame.
10. Stir continuously till all the sauces dry. Remove from fire and serve hot with chilli sauce and chopped chillies in vinegar.

CRISPY NOODLES
Serves -3

INGREDIENTS

100 gms noodles
1/2 tsp garlic paste
1/2 tsp ginger paste
1 sliced onion
1/2 cup sliced capsicum
1 tbsp oil

1 tbsp soya bean sauce
1/4 tsp five-spice powder
1/4 tsp ajinomoto
oil for deep frying
salt to taste
white pepper to taste

METHOD

1. Boil noodles in hot water with 1 teaspoon oil and 1 teaspoon salt.
2. Drain and rinse under tap water.
3. Deep fry in a wok and keep aside.
4. Heat 1 tablespoon oil in a wok and fry ginger and garlic paste.
5. Saute for a second. Add sliced onions and fry for 2 minutes.
6. Add capsicum, salt, pepper, five-spice powder and soya bean sauce. Stir-fry for another minute.
7. Add ajinomoto, mix and remove from fire.
8. Crush the crisp noodles and mix it into the above mixture only at the time of serving.

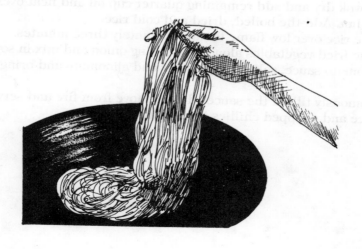

NOODLES WITH SWEET & SOUR SAUCE

Serves - 3

INGREDIENTS

150 gms noodles	2+2 tbsp oil
2 cups vegetable stock	1 tbsp soya bean sauce
1/2 cup chopped spring onion	1/2 cup vinegar
4 pieces cucumber (about 1" each)	5 tbsp tomato sauce
	1 tsp sherry
1/2 cup sugar	1/4 tsp ajinomoto
2 tbsp cornflour	1 tbsp salt
1/4 cup water for cornflour	1 tbsp pepper

METHOD

1. Boil noodles in salted water. Drain off water and wash noodles under tap water.
2. Apply 2 tablespoons oil to prevent them from sticking together.
3. Heat 2 tablespoons oil in a wok and lightly fry noodles for 2 minutes.
4. Add soya bean sauce and remove from fire. Arrange it in a serving dish.
5. Make sauce by mixing sugar, vegetable stock, vinegar, tomato sauce, pepper, salt, ajinomoto and cook on fire for 2 minutes till sugar dissolves. Add sherry to it.
6. Dissolve cornflour in water and add to the above sauce.
7. Cook till the sauce thickens. Add cucumber pieces and spring onion.
8. Remove from fire and pour on the fried noodles at the time of serving.

VEGETABLE RICE NOODLES
Serves - 4

INGREDIENTS

250	gms rice noodles	4	tbsp refined oil
1/4	cup peas	2	tbsp butter
1/4	cup bamboo shoots	2	tbsp soya bean sauce
1/4	cup carrot	2	tbsp vinegar
1/4	cup chopped spring onion	2	tbsp tomato sauce
1	tbsp cornflour		salt to taste
1	tsp ginger paste		pepper to taste

METHOD

1. Soak the rice noodles in warm water for 5 to 7 minutes. Remove from water and keep aside. Do not boil the rice noodles or do not over soak them as they would turn into a paste.
2. Cut carrot and bamboo shoots into long strips and chop spring onion fine.
3. Boil peas and drain off. Keep aside.
4. Grind ginger into a fine paste.
5. Heat 2 tablespoons oil and butter and add the ginger paste along with cut carrot, bamboo shoots, spring onion and boiled peas. Fry for a minute.
6. Add soya bean sauce, vinegar, tomato sauce, salt and pepper to it and cook till the sauces dry.
7. Dissolve cornflour in a quarter cup water and add to the above vegetables.
8. Heat 2 tablespoons oil in another wok and lightly fry the noodles.
9. Mix the vegetable mixture with the noodles at the time of serving or pour the vegetable mixture on noodles as topping.

AMERICAN CHOP SUEY
(WITH VEGETABLES)
Serves - 4

INGREDIENTS

200 gms noodles
1 cup mixed vegetables (thinly sliced)
2 cups vegetable stock
1/2 cup shredded onion
1/2 tsp green chilli paste
1/4 tsp ginger paste
1/4 tsp garlic paste
1/4 tsp sugar
2 tbsp oil
2 tbsp cornflour

2 tbsp butter
1 1/2 cups tomato puree
1/4 cup tomato sauce
1 tbsp soya bean sauce
2 tbsp vinegar
1 tsp white pepper powder
1/4 tsp ajinomoto
oil for deep frying
pinch of orange red colour
salt to taste

METHOD

1. Boil noodles, drain off water and deep fry them. Keep aside.
2. Heat butter in wok. Add cornflour to it and roast well.
3. Add vegetable stock to it.
4. Separately take tomato puree — mix soya bean sauce, tomato sauce, vinegar, sugar and orange red colour to it.
5. Add to the vegetable stock and cook till thick.
6. Remove from fire and keep aside.
7. Heat oil in a saucepan — fry ginger, garlic and green chillies.
8. Add sliced onion to it. Saute for a minute. Then add thinly sliced mixed vegetables to it. Saute for 2 minutes.
9. Mix the vegetables to the prepared sauce as in (1) to (6) above.
10. Arrange the crisp noodles in a serving dish. Pour the vegetable sauce as topping.
11. Serve hot.

VEGETABLE HAKKA CHOW
Serves - 4

INGREDIENTS

100 gms noodles
5-6 thinly sliced beans
1 thinly sliced carrot
1/4 cup thinly sliced cabbage
1/4 cup sliced onion
1/4 cup bean sprout
1/4 cup spring onion stalk

2 tbsp soya bean sauce
2 tbsp vinegar
1/4 tsp ginger juice
3 tbsp oil for vegetables
1 tbsp oil for noodles
1/2 tsp white pepper powder
1/4 tsp ajinomoto
salt to taste

METHOD

1. Boil noodles in 8 cups water and 1/2 teaspoon oil for 2 minutes.
2. Wash the noodles under cold running water. Drain well and sprinkle 1 tablespoon oil to prevent sticking together.
3. Heat 2 tablespoons oil in a wok and fry onion to transparent stage.
4. Add ginger juice and all the thinly sliced vegetables and bean sprout.
5. Saute for 2 minutes, remove from fire.
6. Heat 1 tablespoon oil in another pan and fry the boiled noodles lightly.
7. Mix the fried vegetables to it along with soya bean sauce, vinegar, salt, white pepper and ajinomoto.
8. Stir fry till the sauces dry.
9. Serve hot with chillies in vinegar and chilli sauce.

NOODLES & VEGETABLES IN CORNFLOUR SAUCE

Serves - 3

INGREDIENTS

1	cup mixed sliced vegetables (capsicum, carrot, beans, cabbage)	1	tbsp oil	
		1	tsp soya bean sauce	
		1	tbsp tomato sauce	
1	cup boiled noodles	1	tbsp vinegar	
1	tsp garlic paste	1	tsp capsico sauce	
1	tbsp cornflour	1	tsp chilli sauce	
1/2	tsp sugar		salt to taste	

METHOD

1. Boil noodles in 4 cups water till tender.
2. Drain off water. Wash it under tap water and keep aside.
3. Heat oil in a wok. Saute the garlic, then the mixed vegetables for a minute.
4. Add soya bean sauce, vinegar, capsico sauce, tomato sauce, sugar, salt and chilli sauce and mix well.
5. Mix in the noodles and cook on low flame.
6. Dissolve cornflour in 1/2 cup water and add to the above mixture.
7. Cook till thickened. Serve hot.

VEGETABLE CHOP SUEY

Serves - 4

INGREDIENTS

1	cup mixed thinly sliced vegetables (capsicum, carrot, beans, cabbage)		1	tbsp cornflour
			1	cup water for cornflour
1	cup bean sprout		2	tbsp oil for vegetable
1/2	cup chopped bamboo shoot		2	tsp soya bean sauce
150	gms noodles		1/2	cup tomato sauce
2	sliced onions		1	tsp chilli sauce
1	cup chopped spring onion		2	tbsp vinegar
6	tomatoes for puree		1/2	tsp ajinomoto
1	tsp sugar			oil for deep frying noodles
2	cups vegetable stock			salt to taste
				pepper to taste

METHOD

1. Take 2 tablespoons oil. Stir-fry onion for a minute.
2. Add sliced mixed vegetables, chopped spring onion, chopped bamboo shoots to it and stir-fry for 2 minutes.
3. Add beans sprout to the above mixture and stir-fry for 2 minutes.
4. Make tomato puree and add to the above mixture.
5. Cook till the puree thickens.
6. Add soya bean sauce, vinegar, tomato sauce, chilli sauce, ajinomoto and sugar to the above mixture and cook for 2 minutes.
7. Add a pinch of edible red colour to the cornflour and dissolve cornflour in water.
8. Add dissolved cornflour to the above mixture.
9. Cook till the gravy thickens. Remove from fire and keep aside.
10. Boil noodles in salted water till tender.
11. Drain off water and keep aside.
12. Deep fry noodles, a little at a time to light brown stage.
13. To serve, crush the noodles ring, heat up the prepared sauces and pour on the crushed noodles. Serve hot.

VEGETABLE SPRING ROLLS
Makes - 5 rolls

INGREDIENTS

1	cup flour	2	tsp soya bean sauce
2	eggs *	2	tsp tomato sauce
1	chopped capsicum	2	tbsp vinegar
1/2	cup shredded cabbage	1/2+1/2	tsp ajinomoto
1	tsp chopped celery	1/2	tsp pepper
1/2	cup bean sprout	1	tbsp oil for pancake
1/2	cup bamboo shoots	2	tbsp oil for filling
1	sliced carrot		oil for deep frying
1	chopped onion	1	cup chilled water
1	tsp ginger paste		salt to taste
1/2	tsp garlic paste		

METHOD

1. Mix flour, eggs, chilled water, 1/2 teaspoon ajinomoto, salt and pepper and beat till light and fluffy (could be beaten in a mixie)
2. Make pancakes with a quarter teaspoon oil for 1 pancake in frying pan and keep aside.
3. Heat 2 tablespoons oil in a wok and fry onion till light brown. Add all the vegetables, bean sprouts, bamboo shoots, soya bean sauce, tomato sauce, vinegar, salt, pepper and the other 1/2 teaspoon of ajinomoto.
4. When the sauces dry, remove the wok from the fire and let the cooked vegetables cool completely.
5. Fill the filling in the pancakes and fold it like an envelope.
6. Roll in the same (pancake making) batter and deep fry.

---

* If not using eggs, 1¹/2 cup s water may be added instead of 1 cup water, along with 1/2 teaspoon baking powder.

CAULIFLOWER DUMPLINGS IN SAUCE
Serves - 5

INGREDIENTS

For cauliflower balls
1   cup grated cauliflowers
1/4   cup chopped spring onion
1/2   tsp ginger juice
1   tbsp soya bean sauce
1   cup flour
1   tbsp oil
    salt to taste
    pepper to taste
    pinch of ajinomoto

For the sauce
1   tbsp oil
2   tbsp soya bean sauce
2   tbsp vinegar
1   tbsp cornflour
1/2   cup water for cornflour
1   tbsp chilli sauce
1   tsp garlic paste
1   tsp green chillies paste
    salt to taste
    white pepper to taste

METHOD

1. Mix 1 cup of flour and 1/3 cup hot water and knead well to form a smooth dough.
2. Cover with a damp cloth and keep aside for 10 minutes.
3. Grate the cauliflower. Mix in chopped spring onion, 1 tablespoon oil, ginger juice, soya bean, salt, pepper and a pinch of ajinomoto and mix well.
4. Roll the kneaded dough into small rounds or make a big chappati and cut with round biscuit cutter.
5. Fill with the filling, seal the edges and make pleats.
6. Heat 2 tablespoons oil in a wok and shallow fry the dumplings on slow flame till light brown.

For the sauce

1. Heat oil, fry garlic and green chillies paste to light brown.
2. Add all the sauces along with 2 tablespoons water and mix all.
3. Dissolve cornflour in water and add to the above mixture.
4. Pour this sauce over the dumplings at the time of serving.
5. If the sauce dries, a quarter cup more water could be added and reheated.

STUFFED CAPSICUM IN CHILLI SAUCE

Serves - 4

INGREDIENTS

1 1/2	cup chopped mixed vegetables (carrot, cauliflower, potato, beans, bamboo shoots and spring onion)		1	tbsp chilli sauce
4	green peppers (capsicum)		5	tbsp tomato sauce

1 1/2 cup chopped mixed vegetables (carrot, cauliflower, potato, beans, bamboo shoots and spring onion)
4 green peppers (capsicum)
1/2 cup chopped onion
1/2 tsp ginger paste
1/2 tbsp garlic paste
2 tsp cornflour
1/2 tsp sugar

1 tbsp chilli sauce
5 tbsp tomato sauce
1/4 tsp ajinomoto
4 tbsp oil
1 tbsp chopped parsley leaves
1/2 cup water for cornflour
oil for deep frying
salt to taste
pepper to taste
flour for dusting capsicum

METHOD

1. Heat 2 tablespoons oil in a wok, fry the chopped onion till transparent. Add ginger and garlic and fry for further one minute.
2. Add finely cut vegetables, cook for 5 minutes, add 1/4 cup water. Dry the water completely thus roasting the vegetables to light brown. Add salt to taste and a pinch of ajinomoto. Remove from the wok and keep aside to cool.
3. Cut off tops of capsicum and remove the seeds. Fill with the vegetable mixture, dust the top with flour and deep-fry them. Remove from oil and drain off on a butter paper.
4. Heat remaining 2 tablespoons oil, add tomato sauce, chilli sauce, salt, pepper, sugar and a pinch of ajinomoto to it.
5. Dissolve cornflour in water and add to the above mixture.
6. Cook till the sauces thicken. Add chopped parsley leaves.
7. Arrange the stuffed and fried capsicum in a dish and pour sauce on top.
8. Serve hot.

CAPSICUM & BEAN SPROUT IN GINGER SAUCE

Serves - 5

INGREDIENTS

2	cups chopped capsicum		1	tbsp soya bean sauce
2	cups bean sprout chopped		1	tbsp vinegar
1/2	cup ground onion		1	tsp chilli sauce
1	tsp green chilli paste		1	tbsp tomato sauce
1	cup water or vegetable stock		1/2	tsp ajinomoto
1	tbsp ginger paste			salt to taste
1	tbsp cornflour			white pepper to taste
4	tbsp oil		1½	cups water

METHOD

1. Heat oil in a wok. Add onion paste to it and fry till golden brown. Add ginger paste and green chillies paste.
2. Roast till it leaves the sides of the wok and gets collected in the centre in a ball form.
3. Add chopped capsicum and bean sprout to the above mixture.
4. Mix soya bean sauce, chilli sauce, vinegar, tomato sauce and salt/white pepper with 1/2 cup water and add to the above mixture. Cook till the water dries.
5. Dissolve cornflour in one cup water and add to the above mixture.
6. Cook till a thick gravy is obtained.
7. Serve hot with fried rice or fried soft noodles.

EGG PLANTS IN HOT GARLIC SAUCE
Serves - 4

INGREDIENTS

4	medium sized egg plants
1	cup tomato puree
2	tbsp tomato sauce
1	tbsp onion paste
1	tsp garlic paste
2	tbsp soya sauce
1	tsp vinegar
1	tsp red chilli sauce

1/2	tsp sugar
2	tbsp oil
	oil for deep drying
	salt to taste

(Chinese spices: 1 tsp white pepper powder, 1/4 piece star anise, 1/8 tsp cinnamon, 1/8 tsp clove powder)

METHOD

1. Cut egg plants into square pieces or diagonal pieces or make slanting cuts. Keep them in chilled water for ten minutes.
2. Grind onion and garlic into paste and keep aside.
3. Make tomato puree with 5 medium sized tomatoes and a 1/4 cup water in a mixie. Strain and keep aside.
4. Heat 2 tablespoons oil in a wok and add onion and garlic paste to it.
5. When brown, add tomato puree, tomato sauce, chilli sauce, soya bean sauce, vinegar, sugar, salt to taste and the Chinese spices.
6. Add 1/4 cup water and cook on slow fire.
7. Drain the egg plant from the chilled water. Wipe dry with a napkin and deep fry.
8. Add to the prepared sauce in (5) above and cook on low flame till the sauce thickens to the right consistency.
9. Remove from fire and serve hot.

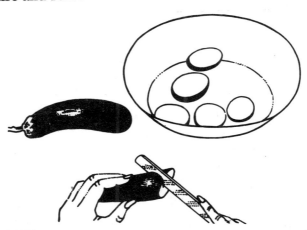

CANTON VEGETABLES IN CREAM SAUCE
Serves - 4

INGREDIENTS

1/2	cup sliced-steamed cauliflower		4	tbsp refined oil
1/2	cup boiled peas		1	tbsp soya bean sauce
1/2	cup chopped spinach leaves		1/4	tsp sugar
1/2	cup chopped tomato		1/2	cup milk
1	tbsp cornflour		1	tbsp sherry
1/2	cup chopped spring onion		1/2	tsp white pepper
1	tbsp butter			salt to taste

METHOD

1. Mix the sliced vegetables with salt, white pepper and sherry and keep aside for 10 minutes.
2. Heat oil and butter in a wok and saute the sliced vegetables mixture along with spring onion for 2 minutes.
3. Add soya bean sauce, sugar and cornflour dissolved in 1/2 cup milk.
4. Mix well, stir fry for 1 or 2 minutes.
5. Serve hot.

FRIED CAPSICUM WITH BEAN SPROUT

Serves - 4

INGREDIENTS

1	cup bean sprout	1/4	tsp ginger paste
2	thinly sliced capsicums	1/4	tsp garlic paste
1	medium onion thinly sliced	1	tsp soya bean sauce
1/4	cup chopped spring onion	1/4	tsp ajinomoto
2	tbsp vegetable stock		salt to taste
2	tbsp oil		pepper to taste

METHOD

1. Soak bean sprout in boiling water for a minute, then wash in cold running water.
2. Heat oil in wok, fry onion to light brown and add ginger and garlic pastes.
3. Add capsicum, spring onion and bean sprout and fry for a minute.
4. Add soya bean sauce, vegetables stock, salt, pepper and ajinomoto.
5. Cook till the sauces and the vegetable stock dry.
6. Remove from fire and serve hot.

STUFFED CUCUMBER
Serves - 4

INGREDIENTS

2	cucumbers	2	tsp cornflour
1	cup scrambled paneer	3	tbsp oil
1	tbsp finely chopped bamboo shoots	1/4	tsp sugar
		$1^1/_2$	tsp soya bean sauce
1/4	cup chopped spring onion	1	tsp capsico sauce
1	cup vegetable stock	2	tbsp tomato sauce
	or	2	tbsp vinegar
1	cup paneer water (whey)	1/4	tsp ajinomoto
1	tsp ground ginger	2	cups chilled water

METHOD

1. Peel the cucumber and cut them in total six portions or sections.
2. Remove the seeds from inside with the help of a scooper or the back of the spoon.
3. Soak in chilled water for 5 minutes.
4. Make paneer and mash it. Add bamboo shoots, spring onion and ginger to it.
5. Add 3/4 tablespoon soya bean sauce, capsico sauce, sugar, 1 tablespoon vinegar, 1 tablespoon tomato sauce, ajinomoto and salt to taste.
6. Stuff this filling in the cucumber pieces.
7. Dust the ends of the cucumber pieces with cornflour to seal them.
8. Heat oil in a wok. Put the cucumber pieces in it and fry for two minutes, turning over on to their sides.
9. Dissolve cornflour in whey water or vegetable stock. Add remaining soya bean sauce, vinegar and tomato sauce to it.
10. Add to the fried cucumber, cover and cook over low heat for 5 minutes.
11. Remove from flame and serve hot.

SPINACH CHINESE STYLE

Serves - 4

INGREDIENTS

500	gms spinach		1/4	tsp soya bean sauce
1	chopped onion		1/8	tsp ajinomoto
1	tsp green chilli paste		1/2	tsp sesame oil
1	tsp garlic paste		2	tbsp oil
1	cup tomato puree		2	tbsp cornflour
1	cup cream			white pepper to taste
1/2	cup spinach water			
	or			
1/2	cup milk			

METHOD

1. Wash spinach and take the leaves and tender stalk.
2. Boil spinach in 1 cup water in a pressure cooker till the whistle.
3. Cool and drain well. Keep the water aside. Grind spinach in a mixie.
4. Heat oil in a wok. Add chopped onion and fry to transparent stage. Add garlic and green chilli paste.
5. Saute for a fraction of a minute. Then add tomato puree. When the puree dries, add the sieved milk cream and mix well.
6. Put in the spinach. Add salt, pepper, sesame oil, ajinomoto and soya bean sauce.
7. Dissolve cornflour in 1/2 cup spinach water or milk and add to the above mixture.
8. Cook till thick consistency is obtained.
9. Remove from fire and serve hot.

STUFFED TOMATOES
Serves - 4

INGREDIENTS

4	tomatoes		1	tbsp oil
1	tbsp soya bean sauce			pinch of ajinomoto
1	cup scrambled paneer			pinch of sugar
1	tbsp tomato sauce			salt to taste
1/2	cup chopped capsicum			pepper to taste
1	tsp vinegar			

METHOD

1. Cut the top of tomatoes and gently scoop out all the pulp.
2. Mix the scrambled paneer with finely chopped capsicum and saute in one tablespoon oil for a minute.
3. Add salt and pepper to taste, soya bean sauce, tomato sauce, ajinomoto, sugar and vinegar.
4. Saute for another minute.
5. Remove from fire, cool it and fill this mixture in tomato and chill it.
6. Cut each tomato petal shaped into five equal petals with the help of a pointed knife.
7. Serve as an open tomato flower with frozen filling in the centre.

RICE NOODLES & VEGETABLES IN CORNFLOUR SAUCE
Serves - 3

INGREDIENTS

1	cup mixed sliced vegetables (capsicum, carrot, beans, cabbage)
100	gms rice noodle
1	tsp garlic paste
1	tbsp cornflour
1/2	tsp sugar

1+1	tbsp oil
1	tsp soya bean sauce
1	tbsp tomato sauce
1	tsp vinegar
1	tsp chilli sauce
	salt to taste

METHOD

1. Boil water and soak rice noodles for 15 minutes.
2. Drain off water and sprinkle 1 tablespoon oil on them.
3. Heat 1 tbsp oil in a wok. Saute garlic paste, then add mixed vegetables for a minute.
4. Add soya bean sauce, vinegar, capsico sauce, tomato sauce, sugar, salt and chilli sauce and mix well.
5. Mix rice noodles and cook on low flame.
6. Dissolve cornflour in 1/4 cup water and add to above mixture.
7. Cook till thickened. Serve hot.

CAULIFLOWER IN SOYA BEAN SAUCE

Serves - 4

INGREDIENTS

1	medium cauliflower	1	tbsp soya bean sauce
1	tsp ginger paste	1	tsp chilli sauce
1	tsp garlic paste	1	tsp 8/8 sauce
1	tsp spice powder	1/4	tsp ajinomoto
1	tsp green chilli paste	1/4	cup water
1	tbsp oil		salt to taste
1	tsp szechuan pepper		pepper powder

METHOD

1. Cut the cauliflower into desired pieces.
2. Marinate the cauliflower in the above sauces, water and spice powder for 3 hours.
3. Cook in the same sauces till all the sauces are dry and cauliflower tender.
4. Heat oil in a wok. Fry ginger and garlic pastes.
5. Add cauliflower to it along with green chilli paste.
6. Cook for 2 minutes and serve hot.

CHINESE FRIED MUSHROOMS
Serves - 4

INGREDIENTS

1	tin mushroom	2	chopped green chillies
	or	1	tbsp soya bean sauce
250	gms fresh mushroom	1/4	tsp ajinomoto
1	cup chopped spring onion	1	tsp salt
3	tbsp oil		

METHOD

1. Wash mushrooms in salted water. Drain and cut into slices. If using tinned mushrooms, cut into slices without washing.
2. Heat oil in a wok. Saute onion. Then add mushrooms. If using fresh mushrooms, add 1/2 cup water to cook the mushrooms.
3. When water dries completely, add salt, soya bean sauce, ajinomoto and chopped green chillies.
4. Mix well for a second and serve hot.

BRAISED CABBAGE
Serves - 4

INGREDIENTS

1	cup mixed vegetables (cauliflower, carrot, beans and peas)
1	small cabbage cut into square pieces
1	cup water
1	small chopped capsicum
1	chopped onion

3	tbsp oil
1/4	tsp ajinomoto
1	tsp soya bean sauce
1	tbsp vinegar
2	tbsp tomato sauce
	salt to taste
	pepper to taste

METHOD

1. Heat oil in a wok. Fry cabbage for 1 minute.
2. Remove cabbage and keep aside.
3. In the same pan, fry capsicum and onion for 2 minutes.
4. Add 1 tablespoon water along with salt, pepper and ajinomoto and cover with a lid on top for 5 minutes, cooking on slow fire.
5. Separately boil mixed vegetables in 3 cups water till 2 cups stock is obtained.
6. Add vegetable stock to the capsicum/onion mixture along with the sauces and cook for 15 minutes on slow flame.
7. Then raise the flame and reduce the gravy to 1 cup.
8. Add butter and remove from fire when the butter dissolves.
9. Arrange the fried cabbage in a serving dish. Pour the sauce on top and serve hot.

CHINESE PICKLED CABBAGE

Serves - 3

INGREDIENTS

1	cup cut cabbage, cut into 2 inches square pieces		4	tbsp sugar
4	tbsp vinegar		4	tbsp tomato sauce
4	tbsp soya bean sauce		1	pod medium garlic
			6	dry red chillies

METHOD

1. Heat up about 2 cups water to boiling point and add the cut cabbage to it for 1 minute covering the container with a lid. .
2. Drain off water and wipe dry the cabbage pieces.
3. Mix vinegar, sugar, soya bean sauce, garlic and red chillies.
4. Grind this mixture to a paste.
5. Add tomato sauce to it and mix well.
6. Mix in the softened cabbage pieces and serve it along with fried rice and noodles.

BRAISED MUSHROOMS
Serves - 4

INGREDIENTS

1	cup button mushrooms		1	tsp ajinomoto
1	cup chopped spring onion		1	piece star anise
1	tbsp soya bean sauce		2	tbsp water
1	tbsp vinegar		2	tbsp oil
1	tbsp tomato sauce			salt to taste
1	tsp white pepper powder			

METHOD

1. Heat oil in a wok.
2. Add mushrooms and stir-fry for 2 to 3 minutes.
3. Add soya bean sauce, vinegar and tomato sauce along with ajinomoto, white pepper powder, star anise and salt to taste.
4. Add water and simmer on slow fire covering the lid for 5 minutes.
5. Before removing from fire, add chopped spring onion and serve hot.
6. Remove and discard star anise before serving.

CHINESE PICKLED CUCUMBER

Serves - 3

INGREDIENTS

1	cup cucumber cut into long strips	1/4	tsp oil
2	tbsp vinegar		pinch of ajinomoto
2	tbsp sugar		pinch of white pepper powder
			1 tsp salt.

METHOD

1. Heat 1/4 teaspoon oil in a wok and fry cucumber pieces for about 1 minute. Remove from wok.
2. In the same wok add salt, sugar, vinegar, ajinomoto and white pepper powder.
3. Remove from fire when the sugar dissolves.
4. Mix in the fried cucumber pieces.
5. Cool and serve.

CAPSICUM BEAN SPROUT CHOP SUEY

Serves - 3

INGREDIENTS

100	gms noodles	1	tbsp tomato sauce
3	sliced capsicum	1+3	tbsp butter
2	cups bean sprout	2	tsp soya bean sauce
1	cup chopped spring onion	1	tsp chilli sauce
1	tbsp chopped celery	2	tbsp vinegar
2	cups vegetable stock	2	tbsp ginger juice
1	tbsp cornflour	1/4	tsp ajinomoto
1	tbsp flour		oil for deep frying noodles

METHOD

1. Heat 1 tablespoon butter in a wok and lightly fry sliced capsicum, celery and spring onion. Add ginger juice and keep aside.
2. Heat 3 tablespoons butter in another wok. Add cornflour and flour to it and roast till light brown.
3. Put off the fire and add vegetable stock.
4. Mix soya bean sauce, vinegar, tomato sauce, chilli sauce to the prepared cornflour sauce. Mix well.
5. Add salt, pepper and ajinomoto. Mix well.
6. Add fried capsicum and bean sprout to the above sauce. Remove from flame and keep aside.
7. Boil noodles in salted water. Drain off water.
8. Deep fry noodles to light brown. Drain on a butter paper and crush them.
9. Arrange the crushed noodles in a serving dish. Pour the hot capsicum - bean sprout sauce on top and serve hot.

ASPARAGUS IN GARLIC SAUCE

Serves - 3

INGREDIENTS

1	tin asparagus (450 ml)		2	tbsp soya bean sauce
1	tsp garlic paste		1	tbsp malt vinegar
1	cup vegetable stock		1	tbsp tomato sauce
1	chopped onion		1	star anise
1	tbsp cornflour			pinch of ajinomoto
1/4	tsp sugar			salt to taste
3	tbsp oil·			pepper to taste

METHOD

1. Drain off the asparagus liquid and cut it into 1 inch slices.
2. Heat oil in a wok. Add chopped onion and garlic paste and saute for a minute.
3. Add asparagus and cook for one more minute.
4. Make cornflour sauce with vegetable stock, add soya bean sauce, vinegar, tomato sauce, sugar, ajinomoto, salt and pepper to it.
5. Pour this sauce over the fried asparagus, add star anise, bring to boil and continue cooking till the sauce thickens.
6. Remove from fire, remove star anise and serve hot.

STUFFED CABBAGE ROLLS

Serves - 3

INGREDIENTS

1	medium cabbage	2	tbsp soya bean sauce
1	cup sliced capsicum	2	tbsp tomato sauce
1	cup sliced carrot	1	tbsp vinegar
1	sliced onion	4	tbsp oil
1/2	cup chopped bamboo shoots	1/4	tsp ajinomoto
1/2	tsp ginger paste		salt to taste
1/2	tsp garlic paste		pepper to taste.
1	tsp sherry		

METHOD

1. Wash the cabbage. Separate leaves and soak them in chilled water for 5 minutes.
2. Heat oil in a wok. Add ginger, garlic pastes and fry for 5 minutes.
3. Add sliced onion. Stir-fry for 2 minutes.
4. Add sliced capsicum, carrot, bamboo shoots. Stir-fry for 5 minutes.
5. Add soya bean sauce, tomato sauce, ajinomoto, vinegar, salt, pepper and sherry. Mix.
6. Remove from fire and cool completely.
7. Place 2 tablespoons of the above mixture into the centre of each cabbage leaf.
8. Fold in the ends of the cabbage leaf and roll it in the shape of spring roll.
9. Serve immediately.

BRAISED EGG PLANT CHINESE STYLE

Serves - 4

INGREDIENTS

3	medium egg plant	3-4	tbsp oil
1	chopped onion	2	tbsp soya bean sauce
1/2	tsp ginger paste	1	tbsp vinegar
1/2	tsp garlic paste	1/4	tsp sugar
1/2	cup vegetable stock		salt to taste
1	tbsp cornflour		pepper to taste

METHOD

1. Heat oil in a wok. Fry the chopped egg plant. Drain and keep aside.
2. In the same oil, add chopped onion, ginger and garlic pastes and fry together for a minute.
3. Add sugar, soya bean sauce and vinegar to it and cook for another minute. Add fried egg plant to it.
4. Dissolve cornflour in 2 tablespoon water. Add vegetable stock to the cornflour. Add salt and pepper.
5. Cover the egg plant mixture with cornflour sauce, lower the flame and simmer on low flame for about 2 minutes till the sauce is thick.
6. Serve hot with boiled or fried rice.

CAULIFLOWER FLORETS IN SAUCE

Serves - 4

INGREDIENTS

1	medium cauliflower cut into thin flat florets	1	egg	
1	tsp ginger paste	1	tsp soya bean sauce	
1	tsp garlic paste	1	tbsp vinegar	
1	tbsp red chilli paste	1	tbsp oil	
1/4	tsp baking powder	1/4	tsp ajinomoto	
2	tbsp flour		oil for deep frying	
1+1	tbsp cornflour		salt to taste	
1	cup vegetable stock for cornflour		pepper to taste	

METHOD

1. Make batter with egg, flour, baking powder, 1 tablespoon cornflour, salt and pepper.
2. Roll cauliflower strips in it and deep fry them. Drain and keep aside.
3. Heat 1 tablespoon oil in a wok . Stir-fry ginger and garlic pastes; add red chilli paste, add soya bean sauce and vinegar and fry for a minute.
4. Add fried cauliflower florets and ajinomoto.
5. Fry till sauce is all around the cauliflower.
6. Dissolve 1 tablespoon cornflour in vegetable stock and add to the above mixture.
7. Cook till the sauce thickens. Serve immediately or cauliflower goes soggy.

MIXED VEGETABLES FRIED

Serves - 3

INGREDIENTS

1/2	cup shredded cabbage		1	tbsp soya bean sauce
1	sliced capsicum		1	tsp vinegar
1	cup bean sprout		1/2	cup vegetable stock
1	sliced onion		3	tbsp oil
1/2	tsp ginger paste			salt to taste
1/2	tsp garlic paste			

METHOD

1. Heat oil in a wok. Fry sliced onion to transparent stage. Add ginger and garlic. Saute for a minute.
2. Add cabbage, capsicum and bean sprout and stir-fry for 2 minutes.
3. Add the vegetable stock, soya bean sauce, vinegar and salt to taste.
4. Cook till sauces dry completely.
5. Serve hot.

FRIED BEAN SPROUTS IN SAUCE

Serves - 4

INGREDIENTS

1	cup bean sprout	1	tbsp soya bean sauce
1	sliced capsicum	1	tbsp vinegar
1/2	cup chopped spring onion	1	tbsp chilli sauce
1	sliced onion	1	tbsp tomato sauce
1/2	tsp ginger ground	1/4	tsp ajinomoto
1	tbsp cornflour		salt to taste
1	cup vegetable stock or water		pepper to taste
3	tbsp oil		

METHOD

1. Soak bean sprout in hot water for 10 minutes. Then wash under cold water tap.
2. Heat oil in a wok, add sliced onion, saute for a minute. Then add ground ginger. Add capsicum, spring onion and bean sprout and fry for a minute.
3. Add soya bean sauce, vinegar, chilli sauce, tomato sauce, salt and pepper to taste and cook for 2 minutes.
4. Dissolve cornflour in vegetable stock or water and add to the above mixture.
5. Bring to boil. Remove from fire and serve hot.

SPINACH IN SWEET & SOUR SAUCE
Serves - 3

INGREDIENTS

For the Spinach
1   kg spinach leaves
1   tbsp oil
     pinch of salt and pepper

For the Sauce
3   tbsp vinegar
1/4 cup water

2   tbsp tomato sauce
1   tsp chilli sauce
2   tbsp sugar
1   tbsp cornflour
1/2 cup water for cornflour
     pinch of ajinomoto
     salt and pepper to taste

METHOD

1.   Wash the spinach leaves, discard the coarse stem.
2.   Steam the spinach on double boiler till soft.
3.   Heat 1 tablespoon oil in a fry pan. Arrange spinach leaves in oil with salt and pepper and leave it on low flame for 2 minutes. Remove from fire.
4.   Make sauce out of water, vinegar, sugar, tomato sauce, and ajinomoto and cook on fire for 2 minutes.
5.   Dissolve cornflour in water and add to the above sauce. Cook the same for a minute till thickened.
6.   Arrange the spinach in a serving bowl and pour the prepared sauce over it.

SWEET AND SOUR VEGETABLES
Serves - 4

INGREDIENTS

2	cups vegetable stock (1/4 cup chopped vegetables boiled in 2 1/2 cups water)	1/2	cup sugar
		5	tbsp tomato sauce
		1	tbsp soya sauce
1	small capsicum	1/2	cup vinegar
1/2	carrot	1/4	tsp ajinomoto
1	inch piece cucumber	1/4	tsp white pepper powder
2 1/2	tbsp cornflour	2	tbsp oil
1/4	cup bamboo shoots	1 1/2	tsp salt

METHOD

1. Take two tablespoons oil in a wok.
2. Add sliced carrot, bamboo shoots and sliced capsicum and fry for a minute.
3. Remove from the wok and keep aside.
4. Combine the soya sauce, vinegar, tomato sauce, sugar, salt, white pepper, ajinomoto and vegetable stock and boil for 5 minutes.
5. Dissolve cornflour in a quarter cup boiled and cooled water and add to the above mixture.
6. Simmer, stirring for two to three minutes till it thickens to the required consistency.
7. Add the fried vegetables and sliced cucumber and remove from fire.
8. Serve hot.

BRAISED BROCCOLI
Serves - 2

INGREDIENTS

250	gms broccoli
1	onion finely chopped
1/4	cup vegetable stock
1/2	tsp chilli sauce
1/2	cup chopped spring onion
1	clove garlic

3	tbsp oil
1	tsp soya bean sauce
1	tsp vinegar
1	tbsp sherry (optional)
	pinch of ajinomoto
	pepper to taste

METHOD

1. Cut broccoli in small florets and put in boiling water for 2 minutes. Drain off water.
2. Heat oil in a wok, add chopped onion and garlic and fry for a minute.
3. Add broccoli, salt and pepper and stir-fry for another minute.
4. Mix vegetable stock, chilli sauce, soya bean sauce, vinegar and sherry and add to the broccoli along with ajinomoto and cover it with a lid on top.
5. Cook on low heat for 5 minutes. Add spring onion stalk and remove from fire and serve hot.

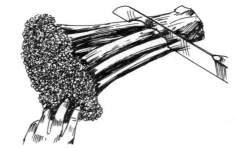

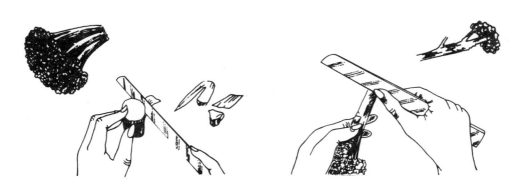

SWEET & SOUR CABBAGE
Serves - 4

INGREDIENTS

1	cup shredded cabbage
2	tsp flour
2	tsp cornflour
4	tbsp breadcrumbs
2-3	tbsp milk (or as required) to make a batter
1/4	tsp baking powder
1/4	tsp ajinomoto
1/4	tsp white pepper powder
	oil for deep frying
	salt to taste

Ingredients for the sauce

1	tsp soya sauce
2	tbsp tomato sauce
2	tbsp tomato puree
1/4	cup vinegar
1	tbsp cornflour
1/4	cup sugar
2	tbsp water to dissolve cornflour

METHOD

1. Make a batter of flour, cornflour, baking powder, ajinomoto, salt, white pepper and milk. Bring to a thick consistency.
2. Add shredded cabbage to it.
3. Bind it into about 6 to 8 oblong shaped pieces.
4. Roll them into breadcrumbs and deep fry.
5. Drain off oil and keep aside on a butter paper.
6. Mix in the sauce ingredients (except cornflour) along with one cup water and boil for five minutes.
7. Dissolve cornflour in two tablespoons water and add to the above sauce in (6).
8. Stir continuously until sauce thickens.
9. Add the fried cabbage to it and serve immediately.

BEAN CURD HOME STYLE

Serves - 5

INGREDIENTS

250 gms bean curd	2 tbsp soya bean sauce
1/4 cup mushroom	1/4 tsp ajinomoto
1/4 cup bamboo shoots	1/2 tsp white pepper powder
2 tbsp cornflour	salt to taste
3 tbsp oil	oil for frying
1/4 cup chopped spring onion	

METHOD

1. Cut the bean curd into 2 inch square pieces and fry in half cup oil till light brown turning very carefully.
2. Remove from hot oil and keep aside on a butter paper.
3. If using fresh mushrooms, remove the stem and cut into small pieces.(If using Chinese mushrooms, soak them in warm water for half an hour.) Remove from water and cut into pieces.
4. Slice bamboo shoots finely.
5. Heat oil, add bamboo shoots, and mushrooms. Stir-fry for 2 minutes and then add fried bean curd and spring onion.
6. Add soya bean sauce, ajinomoto, white pepper powder and salt to taste and mix well.
7. Dissolve cornflour in 3 tablespoons water and add to the above mixture. Mix thoroughly and cook till thickens.

CAUTION

Do not overstir as the bean curd breaks easily.

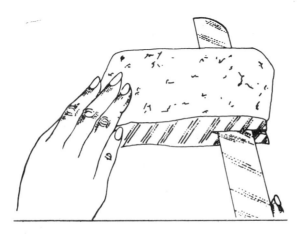

SUPER OMELETTE CHINESE STYLE

Serves - 4

INGREDIENTS

2	eggs	1/2	cup vegetable stock
1	cup beans sprout	1¹/₂	tsp cornflour
1/2	cup sliced tinned mushrooms	1	tbsp soya bean sauce
1	stalk celery	1	tbsp vinegar
1/2	tsp garlic paste	2¹/₂	tbsp oil
1/2	tsp ginger paste		pinch of ajinomoto
1	tbsp chopped onion		salt to taste
1	sliced capsicum		pepper to taste

METHOD

1. Heat 1¹/₄ tablespoon oil in a frying pan over high heat.
2. Add onion, ginger and garlic pastes and fry for a minute.
3. Mix in capsicum, bean sprout, celery and mushrooms and cook for another minute. Add salt to taste and ajinomoto.
4. Remove from fire and keep aside.
5. Take remaining oil in a frying pan on full flame.
6. Beat eggs, adding salt and pepper to taste and make an omelette.
7. Cook for 2 minutes. Remove from fire. Arrange the fried vegetables over it and keep aside.
8. At the time of serving, mix vegetable stock, soya bean sauce, vinegar and cornflour and boil it to make the cornflour sauce.
9. Pour this prepared sauce over the omelette filled with vegetable filling only at the time of serving.

CABBAGE BALLS IN GARLIC SAUCE
Serves - 4

INGREDIENTS

2	cups shredded cabbage
1	tbsp garlic paste
1	tbsp chopped parsley leaves
4	tbsp oil
1	tbsp cornflour
1/2	tsp sugar
1/2	cup chopped onion
1	tsp soya bean sauce
1	tbsp tomato sauce
2	tbsp vinegar
1/2	cup tomato puree

2	cups water
1/2	tsp ajinomoto
	breadcrumbs for coating
	oil for deep frying

For the batter

4	tbsp cornflour
1/4	tsp baking powder
	salt to taste
	water for making batter

METHOD

1. Make a thick paste of cornflour, baking powder, salt and water.
2. Roll finely shredded cabbage in this batter. Roll in breadcrumbs. Make round balls and deep fry to golden brown.
3. Drain and keep aside.
4. Heat oil in a wok. Add chopped onion and saute for a minute.
5. Add garlic paste and fry for another minute.
6. Add salt, tomato sauce, vinegar, soya bean sauce, ajinomoto and sugar to it and cook till the sauce thickens.
7. Add tomato puree and cook for 5 minutes.
8. Dissolve 1 tablespoon cornflour in 2 cups of boiled and cooled water and add to the above mixture.
9. Bring the mixture to boil, lower the flame and cook till the gravy thickens.
10. Add cabbage balls just before serving and garnish with parsley leaves.
11. Serve hot.

EGG FOO YONG

Serves - 4

INGREDIENTS

4	eggs		1	tsp soya bean sauce
1	cup bean sprout		1/4	tsp ajinomoto
1	cup chopped spring onion		4	tbsp oil
1	clove garlic		1-2	Chinese mushrooms
1/2	cup vegetable stock			salt to taste
1/2	tsp ginger paste			pepper to taste
1	tbsp cornflour			

METHOD

1. Heat oil in a wok. Add bean sprout to it. Stir-fry for a minute.
2. Soak mushrooms in hot water for 10 minutes. Then chop them. Add chopped mushrooms, ginger, garlic paste and spring onion to bean sprout.
3. Mix well for a minute.
4. Mix cornflour in vegetable stock and add to the above mixture.
5. Add salt, pepper, ajinomoto and soya bean sauce to it.
6. Bring to boil and cook till the mixture thickens. Remove from fire and keep aside.
7. Beat eggs in a bowl, adding salt to taste.
8. Take oil in a wok, heat it and make an omelette of the egg mixture.
9. Pour thickened sauce over the prepared omelette and serve hot.

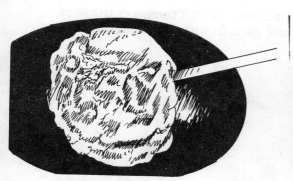
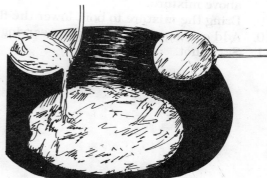

THREE TREASURES
Serves - 4

INGREDIENTS

1	tin asparagus (450 gms)
1	tin mushroom (450 gms)
500	gms spinach
1	chopped onion
4	cloves garlic
2	medium tomatoes
4	tbsp oil ·

1	tbsp soya bean sauce
1/2	tsp sugar
	salt to taste
	pepper to taste

METHOD

1. Drain off liquid from asparagus and mushrooms tins and chop them fine.
2. Wash spinach in running tap water and drain well.
3. Cut off hard stems of spinach and take only the tender stalk and leaves.
4. Heat 2 tablespoons oil in a pan. Add spinach, stir-fry for a minute and remove from fire.
5. In another wok, heat remaining oil, stir-fry peeled and crushed garlic. Add onion and fry for a minute. Add chopped tomatoes, saute for another minute. Then add asparagus and mushrooms.
6. Add 2 cups water, soya bean sauce and sugar. Mix well and bring to boil. Add salt and pepper.
7. Add fried spinach and covering with a lid simmer on medium flame for 10 minutes.
8. Serve hot.

FRIED WONTONS
Serves - 4

INGREDIENTS

For wontons

1/2	cup flour
2	tbsp cornflour
1	egg
	pinch of salt
1	tbsp water

For wonton filling

1	tbsp chopped capsicum
2	tbsp shredded carrot
1	tbsp chopped spring onion stalk
1/8	tsp ajinomoto

1	tbsp oil
	salt and pepper to taste
	oil for deep frying

For the sauce

1	tsp garlic paste
1	tsp green chilli paste
2	tbsp soya bean sauce
2	tbsp vinegar
2	tbsp tomato sauce
1/8	tsp ajinomoto
3	tbsp water

METHOD

1. Mix flour, cornflour, egg and salt and make into a dough.
2. Cover it with damp cloth and keep aside for 15 minutes.
3. For the Filling :
   Heat oil, fry capsicum, carrot, spring onion. Add salt and pepper. Saute for a minute and remove from fire.
4. Roll out Wonton dough into a square about $1^1/_2$", place about 1/4 teaspoon of above filling and fold as shown on page 16.
5. Heat oil in a wok over medium heat and deep fry wontons.
6. Drain on a butter paper.
   For Sauce :
7. In another saucepan, fry garlic and green chillies for a second in 1 teaspoon oil. Add all the sauces, ajinomoto and water.
8. Put back fried wontons in the sauces.
9. If required, make cornflour gravy by dissolving 1 tablespoon cornflour in 1 cup water. Add cornflour gravy to fried wontons and serve hot.

BAKED DISHES

BAKED VEGETABLES CHINESE STYLE

Serves - 5

INGREDIENTS

1	cup small potatoes (whole)		1	tsp ginger paste
1	cup small onion (whole)		3	tbsp butter
1/2	cup peas		3	tbsp oil
1/2	cup chopped carrot		1/4	tsp ajinomoto
250	gms tomatoes		2	tsp chilli sauce
1	tbsp garlic paste		1	tsp soya bean sauce
2	tbsp onion paste			salt to taste

METHOD

1. Boil potatoes, remove skin and keep aside.
2. Boil carrots and peas in minimum quantity of water and let the water dry completely.
3. Peel the small onions and do not boil them.
4. Grind one big onion to paste along with ginger and garlic.
5. Make tomato puree by putting tomatoes in mixie and grinding.
6. Heat oil, fry onion, ginger and garlic to light brown.
7. Add tomato puree along with boiled peeled potatoes, whole small onion, boiled peas and boiled carrots.
8. Roast for 5 minutes, adding a quarter cup water, little by little.
9. Add soya bean sauce, chilli sauce, ajinomoto, salt to taste and cook till all the water and the sauces dry.
10. Transfer it in ovenproof dish, put dots of butter on top and bake in hot oven at 200°C for 10 minutes.

VEGETABLES NOODLE PIE

Serves - 5

INGREDIENTS

1	cup mixed vegetables (chopped carrot, chopped beans, chopped capsicum and finely chopped cauliflower)	1	tbsp flour
100	gms noodles	1	egg*
2	chopped onion	1	tsp chilli sauce
4	chopped green chillies	2	tbsp soya bean sauce
1/2"	piece ginger	2	tbsp tomato sauce
1/4	tsp mustard powder	1	tbsp vinegar
2	tbsp butter	1/2	tsp ajinomoto
1	cup milk	2	tbsp breadcrumbs
		1	tbsp oil for noodles
		1/4	tsp white pepper
			salt to taste

METHOD

1. Boil noodles in hot water in which 1/2 teaspoon salt and 1/2 teaspoon oil is added till the noodles are tender.
2. Drain well and apply oil to noodles to prevent them from sticking together.
3. Steam the mixed vegetables for 2 minutes.
4. Heat butter in a wok. Fry onion and green chillies and saute till onion is transparent. Then add flour to it.
5. Roast the flour and remove from fire. Add milk.
6. Put back on fire till the mixture is thick.
7. Add chopped steamed vegetable along with the boiled noodles.
8. Add mustard powder, soya bean sauce, pepper, ajinomoto, salt, yolk of egg, tomato sauce, vinegar and chilli sauce.
9. Beat the egg white stiff and fold in the above mixture.
10. Pour in an ovenproof dish. Sprinkle breadcrumbs and bake at 200°C till golden brown.

---

* If not using egg, use 1¹/2 cups milk instead of 1 cup and use 1/2 tsp baking powder.

STUFFED BREAD WITH CORN & CAPSICUM

Serves - 5

INGREDIENTS

1	400 gms unsliced bread		1	cup milk
1	chopped onion		2	tbsp tomato sauce
1	cup chopped capsicum		2	tbsp vinegar
1	cup sweet corn cream		1/2	cup tomato puree
1	cup bean sprout		1	tbsp soya bean sauce
1	cup chopped spring onion		1	tsp chilli sauce
2	stalks chopped celery		1/2	cup oil
2	tbsp butter			salt to taste
2	tbsp cornflour			white pepper to taste

METHOD

1. Cut the bread horizontally and remove the slice from the top.
2. Scoop out the centre crumbs of bread with a spoon and leave one inch border all round.
3. Smear butter all round the bread and bake at 200°C for five minutes in a pre-heated oven.
4. Heat oil in wok, fry chopped onion for a while. Then add chopped capsicum, spring onion, bean sprout and celery. Saute for a minute.
5. Add tomato puree and cook till the puree thickens.
6. Add sweet corn cream, soya bean sauce, vinegar, tomato sauce, chilli sauce, salt and pepper to taste.
7. Dissolve cornflour in milk and cook on fire to required thickness.
8. Add the cornflour to the corn/capsicum mixture and mix well.
9. Pour the above mixture into the baked bread case and close with the removed top slice.
10. Rebake for five minutes before serving.

CORN AND CHEESE BAKE

Serves -5

INGREDIENTS

1	tin sweet corn cream	1	tsp szechuan pepper
3	cubes cheese	1	tbsp soya bean sauce
8	bread slices	1/2	tsp ajinomoto
1	cup chopped spring onion	1	cup milk for soaking bread
1	tbsp butter		salt to taste
1/2	tsp garlic paste		white pepper to taste
1	tsp dry red chilli paste		

METHOD

1. Melt butter in a wok. Saute the chopped onions to transparent stage. Add red chilli paste and garlic paste.
2. Cook for a second, then add tinned corn, spring onion , grated cheese and salt to taste.
3. Add soya bean sauce, ajinomoto, szechuan pepper paste and cook till the mixture is completely dry.
4. Remove the crust of bread and cut it into any fancy shapes or leave it as a square piece. Soak in milk, remove carefully and arrange it in a greased baking tin.
5. Apply the above mixture over it and sprinkle breadcrumbs.
6. Bake at 200°C for 10 to 15 minutes.
7. Serve hot with chilli sauce.

CHINESE NOODLES BAKE
Serves-2

INGREDIENTS

100	gms noodles	1/2	tbsp cornflour
1	cup Chinese mushroom	1	tbsp soya bean sauce
1	cup sliced celery and	2	tbsp oil
	spring onion cut into bits		pinch of five spice powder
1/2	cup of vegetable stock		salt to taste
1	clove pounded garlic		pepper to taste

METHOD

1. Boil noodles, drain water and ~~~ apply oil. Keep aside.
2. Heat 2 tables~~~ ~~~espoons oil in a wok. Fry garlic. Add washed, sliced mushrooms and celery/spring onion mixture and stir-fry for another 3 minutes.
3. Add soya bean sauce, salt and pepper to taste, five spice powder and cornflour dissolved in water to above mixture.
4. Arrange noodles on a greased baking dish and pour the filling as in (2) and (3) above as toppings.
5. Bake at 200°C in a preheated oven for 10 minutes.

BAKED RICE WITH CAPSICUM AND BEAN SPROUT

Serves - 5

INGREDIENTS

2	cups boiled rice		1/2	tbsp sugar
2	chopped capsicums		1	tsp garlic paste
1/2	cup bean sprout		1	tsp ginger paste
2	chopped onions		1/4	cup tomato sauce
2	chopped tomatoes		2	tbsp vinegar
1/2	cup cashewnut powder		1	tsp chilli sauce
2	cheese cubes		2	tbsp soya bean sauce
1/2	cup oil		1/2	tsp ajinomoto
1	cup water or vegetable stock			salt to taste
1	tbsp cornflour			

METHOD

1. Heat oil in a wok. Add onions and fry to transparent stage.
2. Add chopped tomatoes, cashewnut powder, chopped capsicums and bean sprout and saute for two minutes.
3. Add soya bean sauce, vinegar, tomato sauce, chilli sauce, ajinomoto and sugar and mix well.
4. Add boiled, dried and mashed rice to it and mix well.
5. Dissolve cornflour in one cup water or vegetable stock and add to the above mixture.
6. Cook till cornflour thickens around the vegetables and rice.
7. Put in a greased pie dish and sprinkle grated cheese over it.
8. Bake at 200°C for twenty minutes.

BAKED BROCCOLI IN SOYA BEAN SAUCE

Serves - 4

INGREDIENTS

500	gms broccoli	2	tbsp breadcrumbs
1	cup water for boiling broccoli	2	tbsp soya bean sauce
1	chopped onion	2	tbsp oil
1	tbsp green chilli paste	1	tbsp flour
1	cup chopped spring onion	1	star anise
2	tbsp butter		pinch of ajinomoto
			pepper to taste

METHOD

1. Heat oil and 1 tablespoon butter in a wok and fry onion till transparent.
2. Add flour to it and roast well. Lower flame.
3. Add 1 cup water, pepper, soya bean sauce, ajinomoto, green chilli paste and star anise.
4. Cut and separate broccoli in florets. Boil in 1 cup water for 2 minutes.
5. Add to onion - soya bean sauce mixture and mix well.
6. Cook till completely dry. Remove star anise.
7. Pour in a greased container. Put dots of butter on top. Sprinkle breadcrumbs over it and bake at 200°C preheated oven for 20 minutes.

Note: No salt added to this dish. If salt is less, season well with soya bean sauce before baking.

PINEAPPLE BAKE WITH NOODLES

Serves - 4

INGREDIENTS

1	cup boiled noodles
1/2	cup chopped pineapple slices
1/2	cup boiled chopped potatoes
1/2	cup boiled chopped carrot
1/2	cup sliced capsicum
1	cup milk
1	cup cream
2	tbsp butter
1	tsp soya bean sauce
1	tbsp tomato sauce
1	tbsp vinegar

2	tbsp flour
1	tsp dry red chilli paste
	salt to taste
	pepper to taste

For the topping

2	tbsp butter
3	tbsp breadcrumbs
2	tbsp grated cheese
3	tbsp crushed cheese biscuits

METHOD

1. Melt butter in a wok, add flour to it and fry till light brown.
2. Lower the flame and add milk, stirring continuously.
3. Add cream to it. Also add boiled chopped vegetables and mix well.
4. Add soya bean sauce, tomato sauce, vinegar and dry red chilli paste to it along with salt and pepper.
5. Add the boiled noodles and chopped pineapple slices to it. Remove from fire and cool.
6. Mix the topping materials and mash well.
7. Spread the noodles and other mixture on a greased pie dish. Spread the topping on top of it.
8. Bake at 200°C for 20 minutes.

BAKED CORN CHINESE STYLE
Serves - 3

INGREDIENTS

250	gms fresh corn or	25	gms (1 cube) cheese
1½	cups tinned corn	1½	cup milk
1	cup chopped spring onion	1	tsp soya bean sauce
3	tbsp butter	1	tsp szechuan pepper
2	tbsp cornflour	1/4	tsp ajinomoto
1/2	cup cream		salt to taste

METHOD

1. Heat butter in a wok. Add cornflour and roast to light brown.
2. Lower the flame, add milk stirring continuously till a thick consistency is obtained.
3. In another frying pan, take corn, cream, cheese, salt, pepper and ajinomoto.
4. Cook for a minute and add soya bean sauce to it.
5. Mix in spring onion to the corn mixture and stir well.
6. Arrange the corn mixture in a greased container.
7. Pour sauce as topping.
8. Spread grated cheese over this.
9. Bake at 200°C for 10 minutes till light brown.

BAKED RICE IN SAUCE
Serves-4

INGREDIENTS

150 gms rice
6 tomatoes
1 chopped onion
25 gms cheese (1 cube)
1/2 tsp ginger paste
1/2 tsp garlic paste
1 tsp green chilli paste
2 tbsp butter

1/2 tsp sugar
1 tsp soya bean sauce
1 tbsp cornflour
1½ cup water for cornflour
2 tbsp breadcrumbs
salt to taste.
pepper to taste

METHOD

1. Boil rice in salted water with 1/2 teaspoon salt and 1/2 teaspoon oil.
2. Drain off water and leave to dry.
3. Heat butter in a saucepan, fry chopped onion, saute for a minute. Add ginger and garlic pastes.
4. Add tomato puree made out of 6 tomatoes, green chilli paste and soya bean sauce and cook for 2 minutes.
5. Add grated cheese, sugar, cornflour dissolved in water, salt and pepper.
6. Cook till sauce thickens.
7. Arrange boiled dried rice in a greased baking dish.
8. Pour sauce on top.
9. Sprinkle breadcrumbs and bake at 200°C till light brown on top.

CHILLI NOODLES BAKE

Serves-5

INGREDIENTS

For the chilli sauce

8	dry red chillies
1	pod garlic (15 flakes)
½	tsp cumin seed
½	cup vinegar
½	cup tomato ketchup*
1	tsp sugar
½-1	tsp salt

For the noodles

150	gms boiled noodles
1	tbsp cornflour
1	cup hot water or tomato puree
2	tbsp oil
	salt and pepper to taste

For the semolina

1¹/²	cup suzi (semolina)
2	chopped onions
2	chopped green chillies
2	tbsp chopped mint leaves
2	tbsp coriander leaves paste
½	tsp garlic paste
½	tsp ginger paste
1	cup milk or water
2	salt to taste
	pepper to taste
	garnish with 1 tbsp butter and 25 gms cheese (1 cube cheese)

METHOD

1. Grind the ingredients for chilli sauce and keep aside.
2. Boil noodles in 4 cups salted water. Drain off water and keep aside.
3. Take two tablespoons oil and fry the boiled noodles. Dissolve cornflour in water and add to it. Then add tomato puree and salt/pepper.
4. Cook till the puree thickens, remove from fire.
5. Heat two tablespoons oil again; fry chopped onion to transparent stage.
6. Add ginger paste and garlic paste and then add semolina.
7. Roast semolina to light brown stage. Then add coriander leaves, mint leaves paste, salt and pepper.
8. Pour water or milk and keep stirring till thick.

Assembling

1. Grease an ovenproof dish.
2. Arrange the semolina layer in the dish.
3. Spread the chilli sauce on top of semolina layer.
4. Arrange the noodle layer on top of the chilli sauce layer.
5. Put dots of butter and grated cheese as garnish topping.
6. Bake at 200°C for 10 minutes till light brown.

* If using Tomoto sauce increase the sugar quantity to 2 tbsp in place of 1 tsp.

MUSHROOM AND CAPSICUM BAKE

Serves - 4

INGREDIENTS

1	tin button mushrooms or		1	tbsp green chillies paste
250	gms fresh mushrooms		3	tbsp cornflour
1	cup chopped capsicum		1	tbsp flour
1/2	cup chopped onion		5	tbsp butter
1	stalk chopped celery		2¹/₂	cups milk
1/2	tsp garlic paste			salt to taste
1/2	tsp ginger paste			pepper to taste

METHOD

1. Take two tablespoons butter in a wok and saute the chopped tinned mushrooms for a minute.
2. Add chopped capsicum to it along with chopped celery. Add salt and pepper to taste.
3. Take three tablespoons butter in another wok, fry ginger and garlic pastes. Add chopped onion till transparent.
4. Add cornflour and flour to it and cook till well roasted.
5. Lower the flame and add milk, stirring continuously.
6. Add salt and pepper to taste and green chillies paste.
7. Cook for 5 minutes till the sauce gets quite thick.
8. Mix this sauce with the mushroom - capsicum mixture.
9. Pour in a greased tin and sprinkle breadcrumbs on top.
10. Bake at 200°C for ten minutes.

Note: If using fresh mushrooms chop them in cubes and boil in water for 5 minutes. Drain off water and use as required.

CORN NOODLE BAKE

Serves - 4

INGREDIENTS

1	cup boiled noodles	2	tbsp butter
1	cup sweet corn cream or	1	tsp butter as topping
1	cup boiled fresh corn	1	tsp soya bean sauce
1	chopped onion	2¹/₂	tbsp tomato sauce
1	chopped green chilli	1	tbsp vinegar
1	tsp garlic paste	1	tsp sugar
5	tomatoes	1/4	tsp ajinomoto
1	tsp dry red chilli paste		salt to taste
1	tbsp cornflour		pepper to taste
25	gms cheese (1 cube)		

METHOD

1. Boil noodles in 6 cups of water with 1/2 teaspoon salt and 1/2 teaspoon oil till tender.
2. Drain off water and wash under tap water.
3. Boil corn (3 fresh cobs) in 4 cups water in a pressure cooker for 5 minutes after whistle.
4. Cool, remove the corn grains and keep aside (or take tinned corn).
5. Heat butter in a wok. Add chopped onion and saute for a minute. Then add garlic paste and chopped green chillies. Let the garlic turn brown.
6. Make puree out of tomatoes and add to the onion and cook for 2 minutes.
7. Add red chilli paste, soya bean sauce, ajinomoto, vinegar, tomato sauce, sugar, salt and pepper to taste.
8. Add the boiled noodles and corn to the above mixture and stir well for 2 minutes.
9. Dissolve cornflour in 2 tablespoons water and add to the above mixture.
10. Bring to the thickened stage.
11. Pour the above mixture in a greased dish. Put dots of butter on top. Sprinkle grated cheese on top.
12. Bake at 200°C for 10 minutes.

BAKED RICE NOODLES WITH SPINACH

Serves - 5

INGREDIENTS

50	gms rice noodles	$1^1/_2$	cups milk
1/2	kg spinach	1	tsp soya bean sauce
1	chopped onion	1	tsp chilli sauce
50	gms grated cheese	1+1	tbsp cornflour
1/4	cup cream	1	tbsp flour
1+2 tbsp butter			salt to taste
6	tomatoes for puree		pepper to taste

METHOD

1. Wash and cut spinach and add 1/2 cup water to it.
2. Cook in a wok till soft. Cool and grind in a mixie to puree stage.
3. Make tomato puree in the mixie and mix with spinach puree. Put wok back on flame.
4. Add cream, salt and pepper to it. Mix well and add one tablespoon cornflour dissolved in one tablespoon water. Cook till thick. Remove from fire.
5. Melt butter in another wok. Mix one tablespoon cornflour and flour and roast for 1 minute.
6. Lower flame and add milk stirring continuously. Cook till thick.
7. Soak the rice noodles in boiled hot water for 20 minutes.
8. Drain off water and add pepper, soya bean sauce and chilli sauce to the noodles.
9. Spread the spinach tomato puree layer in a greased container.
10. Spread the noodle layer on top of this layer.
11. Arrange the prepared sauce (in 5 above) as topping.
12. Sprinkle grated cheese and put dots of butter (1 tablespoon).
13. Bake at 200°C for 15 minutes.

BAKED BROCCOLI WITH VEGETABLES

Serves - 5

INGREDIENTS

2	cups (about 500 gms) broccoli chopped	1	tbsp soya bean sauce	
4	finely chopped tomatoes	4	tbsp tomato sauce	
1	finely chopped capsicum	1/2	cup crushed cashewnuts	
2	finely chopped onion	1/2	cup breadcrumbs	
4	chopped green chillies	1/4	tsp ajinomoto	
1/2	tsp sugar		salt to taste	
4	tbsp butter		white pepper to taste	

METHOD

1. Boil broccoli in 1 cup water for 5 minutes.
2. Heat butter in a wok, add onion and fry till transparent. Add broccoli.
3. Add capsicum, breadcrumbs, green chillies, tomatoes,cashewnuts and salt/white pepper.
4. Add soya bean sauce, tomato sauce, ajinomoto and sugar and mix well for 2 minutes.
5. Remove from fire. Pour into a greased tin and press evenly.
6. Put dots of butter (about 1 tablespoon as topping).
7. Bake at 200°C in preheated oven for 20 minutes. Sprinkle additional 2 tablespoons breadcrumbs as topping, if required.

PARTY SNACKS & PUDDINGS

CAULIFLOWER MANCHURIAN
Serves - 5

INGREDIENTS

1¹/₂	cups grated cauliflower		1/4	cup milk
1	cup chopped spring onion		2	tsp soya bean sauce
2	tsp flour		1	tbsp tomato sauce
2	tsp cornflour		2	tbsp vinegar
1/2	tsp baking powder		1/4	tsp ajinomoto
1/2	tsp pounded garlic			salt to taste
4	chopped green chillies			breadcrumbs for rolling
1	tsp dry red chilli paste			oil for deep frying
2	tbsp oil			

METHOD

1. Make a thick batter of flour, cornflour, baking powder, 1/8 teaspoon ajinomoto, red chilli paste, salt and 1/4 cup milk or 1 egg.
2. Add grated cauliflower to it.
3. Make round balls. Roll in breadcrumbs and deep fry them.
4. Remove cauliflower balls from oil and keep on a butter paper.
5. Heat 2 tablespoon oil in a wok. Stir-fry garlic and green chillies.
6. Add all the sauces to it and mix well.
7. Add the cauliflower balls and salt to taste.
8. Cook till the sauce thickens all round the cauliflower balls.
9. Add chopped spring onion and remaining 1/8 teaspoon ajinomoto.
10. Remove from fire and serve hot.

ONION PANCAKE
Serves - 4

INGREDIENTS

For the pancake

1	cup flour
1/3	cup hot water
1	tbsp refined oil
	pinch of salt
	pinch of ajinomoto
2	tbsp flour to sprinkle

For the filling

2	cups spring onion
1	chopped onion
1/2	tsp garlic paste

1/2	tsp ginger paste
2	tbsp oil
1	tsp soya bean sauce
2	tbsp vinegar
2	tbsp tomato sauce
1	tbsp 8/8 sauce
1/4	tsp ajinomoto
1	tbsp cornflour
1/4	cup water
	salt and white pepper to taste
	oil for deep frying

To make pancakes

1. Knead flour with water to a soft dough, adding salt and ajinomoto.
2. Cover with damp cloth and keep aside for 1/2 hour.
3. Roll out into a 2 inches diameter thin circle with a rolling pin.
4. Apply oil over rolled piece, sprinkle flour.
5. Roll out another piece of dough into 2 inches and place over previous rolled dough.
6. Likewise place 2 more such pieces of dough, applying oil between each layer and sprinkling flour, thus making 4 layers of rolled dough like a sandwich.
7. Re-roll these four layers into about 7 inches diameter circle.
8. Cook on hot ungreased skillet or tawa for a minute turning over quickly until very light brown.
9. Remove from heat and separate each sandwich into thin pancakes.
10. Cut off stiff corners with sharp knife and cover with a damp cloth.
11. Place 4 tablespoons filling on each pancake and fold as shown on page 16. Roll in cornflour batter and deep fry at the time of serving.

To make filling

1. Heat oil in a wok, fry chopped onion for 1 minute.
2. Add ginger and garlic pastes and fry for another minute.
3. Add chopped spring onion, saute for a minute.
4. Add all sauces, salt and pepper and dry sauces completely.
5. Cool and fill in the pancakes (as in 11 above — cornflour to be dissolved in 1/4 cup water).

MIXED VEGETABLE FRITTERS
Serves -4

INGREDIENTS

1	cup mixed vegetables (shredded cabbage, chopped spring onion, chopped onion, bean sprouts)	1/2	tsp ginger paste
		1	tsp soya bean sauce
		1/2	tsp ajinomoto
		1	tsp pepper
1	egg white*		pinch of baking powder
1	tbsp flour		breadcrumbs for coating
2	tbsp cornflour		oil for deep frying
1	tsp green chillies paste		salt to taste
2	tbsp rava (semolina)		

METHOD

1. Mix together soya bean sauce, salt, green chillies, pepper and a quarter teaspoon ginger paste and ajinomoto.
2. Marinate the shredded vegetables and chopped onion in this mixture for 15 minutes.
3. Make a thick batter with flour, cornflour, salt, baking power, ginger and egg white.
4. Add the vegetables mixture to the above batter.
5. Add rava and make into flat round tikkis.
6. Coat with the breadcrumbs.
7. Deep fry to golden brown.

---

*   If not using egg, make the batter with milk and also add half teaspoon baking powder.

CHILLI POTATO
Serves -5

INGREDIENTS

250	gms small potatoes		1/2	tsp ajinomoto
1/2	tsp green chilli paste		2	tbsp oil
1	tsp dry red chilli paste		1/4	tsp white pepper powder
1	tsp garlic paste		1/4	tsp tandoori colour (orange red powder)
2	tbsp soya bean sauce			salt to taste
1	tbsp vinegar			
2	tbsp tomato sauce			

METHOD

1. Peel potatoes and prick them with a fork.
2. Mix the soya bean sauce, vinegar, tomato sauce, one tablespoon oil, salt, white pepper and tandoori colour.
3. Soak the potatoes in the above mixture for three hours.
4. Steam the above mixture and potatoes till tender.
5. Heat the remaining one tablespoon oil, fry garlic and green chilli paste. Add red chilli paste along with a quarter cup water and cook for a minute.
6. Add the cooked potatoes to this mixture and add ajinomoto.
7. Dry the sauces and serve dry and hot.
8. If gravy is required, dissolve one tablespoon cornflour in one cup boiled and cooled water and add to the above mixture. Cook till the gravy thickens.

CRISPY FRIED VEGETABLES
Serves -4

INGREDIENTS

2	cups vegetables (cauliflower pieces, chopped capsicum, sliced brinjal, skinned and sliced potato)	1	egg (optional) or required milk to make into a paste	
1	tsp soya bean sauce for vegetables	1	tsp soya bean sauce	
1	tsp sherry (optional)	1	tsp capsico sauce	
3	tbsp cornflour	1/4	tsp ajinomoto	
2	tbsp flour		salt to taste	
			white pepper to taste	
			oil for deep drying	

METHOD

1. Soak thinly sliced vegetables in 1 teaspoon soya bean sauce and sherry (optional) for 10 minutes.
2. Make thick batter with cornflour, flour, 1 teaspoon soya bean sauce, capsico sauce, salt, white pepper and egg or milk.
3. Roll the soaked vegetables in the above batter and deep fry to golden brown.

GOLDEN FRIED BREAD

Serves - 4

INGREDIENTS

10	slices of bread	1	tsp capsico sauce
1	cup sweet corn cream	1/4	tsp ajinomoto
2	tbsp flour	2	tbsp oil
2	medium onions chopped		oil for deep frying
1	tsp green chilli paste		salt to taste
1	tbsp chilli sauce		pepper to taste
1	tsp soya bean sauce		

METHOD

1. Steam the bread for 1 minute and roll out with a rolling pin.
2. Cut it into three strips.
3. Heat oil, fry chopped onions and green chillies.
4. Add corn to it along with soya bean sauce, chilli sauce, salt, pepper and ajinomoto.
5. Cook till such time that the filling completely dries. Remove from fire and let it cool.
6. Fill the bread strips with filling.
7. Make a paste of flour with one tablespoon water.
8. Seal the filled bread pieces with the paste and roll them in the flour paste well.
9. Deep fry to golden brown.

FRIED CORN CHINESE STYLE
Serves -4

INGREDIENTS

4	corncobs		1/4	tsp ajinomoto
2¹/₂	tbsp flour		1	tsp soya sauce
2¹/₂	tbsp cornflour		1	tbsp vinegar
2	eggs			salt to taste
1/4	tsp baking powder			white pepper to taste
1/2	tsp ginger paste			

METHOD

1. Boil corncobs in a pressure cooker in enough water to cover the corn till the whistle.
2. Continue boiling for ten minutes after the first whistle.
3. Remove from fire and let the pressure drop by itself.
4. Remove (scrape off with knife) the corns from the cobs while hot and leave to cool.
5. Mix them to the lightly beaten egg, flour, cornflour, baking powder, ajinomoto, salt/pepper to taste. Add ginger paste to it and mix well.*
6. Mix in soya sauce and vinegar to the above batter.
7. Heat oil, drop a tablespoon each of the mixture in (6) above to the hot oil till it reaches the golden brown look.
8. Remove on a butter paper.
9. Serve hot with chilli sauce.

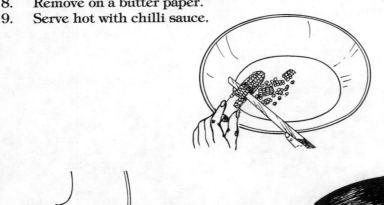

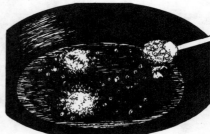

*   More cornflour could be added if batter is not **thick** enough.

POTATO PEAS FRITTER
Serves - 4

INGREDIENTS

1/2 cup boiled and mashed potatoes

1/2 cup boiled and mashed peas

1 egg

1/4 cup cornflour
pinch of baking powder

1 tsp chilli sauce
pinch of ajinomoto

1 tsp ground green chillies
salt and white pepper to taste
oil for deep frying

METHOD

1. Mix mashed potatoes and peas and season the mixture with salt and pepper and keep aside.
2. In a mixing bowl, combine egg,* cornflour, baking powder, salt, pepper, green chilli paste and chilli sauce.
3. Mix well and add the mashed potatoes-peas mixture in this batter.
   (Batter should be so thick that after mixing the potatoes-peas mixture, you are able to make round balls.)
4. Heat oil in a wok and fry round balls to golden brown.
5. Drain on a butter paper.
6. Serve hot with tomato sauce.

* If not using egg, make a thick batter with required quantity of milk and a quarter teaspoon baking powder.

SALT & PEPPER CASHEWNUTS

Serves -4

INGREDIENTS

1	cup cashewnuts		1	tsp cornflour
1	capsicum			oil for deep frying
1/4	cup celery		2	tbsp oil
1	medium onion		1	tbsp soya sauce
1/2	cup spring onion		1/4	tbsp szechuan pepper
1	tbsp chopped green chillies		1/4	tsp sugar
1	tsp ginger paste			salt to taste

METHOD

1. Heat oil in a wok and deep fry the cashewnuts to light golden brown.
2. Remove from oil and keep aside on a butter paper.
3. Chop capsicum fine. Chop celery into small square pieces and also chop spring onion.
4. Heat two tablespoons oil in a wok. Add ginger paste and chopped onion. Saute till onion is transparent. Add cornflour.
5. Add chopped capsicum, celery and spring onion, and fry for two minutes.
6. Add salt to taste, szechuan pepper, sugar and soya bean sauce. Mix in the fried cashewnuts.
7. Cook till the sauce thickens and the mixture is bound well and completely dry.
8. Remove from heat and serve hot.

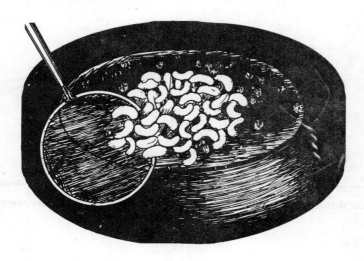

CHEESE IN CHINESE BATTER

Serves -4

INGREDIENTS

50	gms (2 cubes) cheese		1/2	tsp soya bean sauce
50	gms butter		1	tsp capsico sauce
50	gms flour		1/2	tsp ajinomoto
2	eggs		100	ml water
1	grated onion			oil for deep frying
3	ground green chillies			

METHOD

1. Boil butter and water in a frying pan. When it boils, add flour. Stir for a second and remove from fire.
2. Add eggs and beat with an egg beater.
3. Squeeze out the juice of the onion. Add onion and ground green chillies to above mixture.
4. Add soya bean sauce, capsico sauce, grated cheese and ajinomoto.
5. Take a spoonful of this mixture. Pour in hot oil and deep fry to light brown.
6. Serve hot.

POTATO BULLETS
Serves -4

INGREDIENTS

1	cup boiled mashed potatoes	1	tsp soya bean sauce
1/2	cup peas	1	tsp worcestershire sauce
1	chopped onion	1/2	tsp ajinomoto
2	bread slices	1	tsp white pepper
6	tbsp cornflour		oil for deep frying
1	egg (optional)		salt to taste

METHOD

1. Boil the potatoes, peel and mash
2. Boil peas and add to the potatoes.
3. Add chopped onion to the above mixture and mix well.
4. Add soaked,dried and mashed bread slices, egg, worcestershire sauce, soya bean sauce, ajinomoto, salt and pepper and mix well. Add two tablespoon cornflour to it.
5. Roll the mixture in remaining cornflour and make bullet shaped pieces.
6. Deep fry in hot oil till light brown.

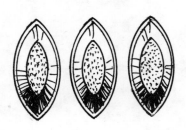

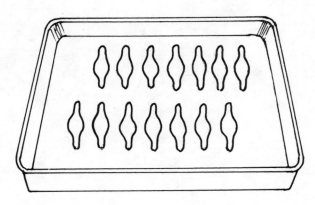

CHEESE TOAST
Serves -4

INGREDIENTS

10	bread slices
1	cup flour
50	gms (2 cubes) cheese
2	eggs* (optional)
1/2	tsp baking powder

1/2 tsp spice powder
1 tsp soya bean sauce
pinch of salt
oil for deep frying

METHOD

1. Make a thick batter with flour, eggs and baking powder. Beat it with an egg beater or in a mixie till light and fluffy.
2. Add grated cheese to it along with soya bean sauce and pinch of salt. Add spice powder.
3. Cut away the crust of bread and cut each slice into equal squares.
4. Apply the above batter on each square of bread only on one side.
5. Heat oil and deep fry the bread squares keeping the cheese side down.
6. Remove from oil on a grease-proof paper and serve hot.

* If not using egg make thick batter with milk.

PLAIN BURGER SUPREME

Serves -5

INGREDIENTS

1	cup mixed vegetables (peas, chopped carrot, chopped beans).
5	plain buns
1/2	cup boiled chopped potatoes
1/2	cup chopped capsicum
1	tbsp flour
1	tbsp cornflour
2	tbsp breadcrumbs

3	tbsp butter
2	tbsp tomato sauce
1	tsp soyabean sauce
1	tbsp worcestershire sauce
2	tbsp vinegar
1	tsp szechuan pepper
1/4	tsp ajinomoto
	salt to taste

METHOD

1. Keep the buns in the refrigerator for two hours.
2. Cut the top of the bun and scoop out the inner portion of the buns.
3. Boil the mixed vegetables in one cup water with 1/2 teaspoon salt till tender and the water is completely dry.
4. Mix the boiled vegetables to chopped capsicum and boiled chopped potatoes.
5. Heat butter in a saucepan and add flour and cornflour to it.
6. Roast the flour and cornflour, lower the flame. Add milk, stirring continuously.
7. Cook till the sauce thickens. Add soya bean sauce, chilli sauce, vinegar, worcestershire sauce, tomato sauce, szechuan pepper, ajinomoto and salt to taste.
8. Add the boiled vegetables to it along with potatoes and capsicum. Remove from fire and cool.
9. Fill the buns with this filling.
10. Sprinkle breadcrumbs on top. Put a dot of butter on top of breadcrumbs and bake at 200°C for ten minutes.

PEAS ROLLS
Serves -5

INGREDIENTS

1	cup boiled mashed peas
1/2	cup rava (semolina)
2	chopped onions
1/4	tsp sugar
3	tbsp oil
1	tbsp chopped parsley leaves
1	tsp soya bean sauce
1	tsp chilli sauce

1	tsp vinegar
	oil for deep frying
	salt to taste

For the flour

1   cup flour, 1/4 tsp baking powder, 2 slices bread, water to knead dough, salt to taste

METHOD

1. Take flour, add baking powder to it and sieve together.
2. Soak bread slices in water. Squeeze out water, mash and mix with the flour.
3. Make dough with water and keep it aside covering with a damp cloth.
4. Take oil in a wok, fry onion to transparent stage, add rava to it and roast to light brown stage.
5. Add peas, soya bean sauce, chilli sauce, vinegar, sugar and salt to taste and mix well.
6. Saute for a minute. Then add parsley leaves.
7. Remove from fire and cool.
8. Take a ball of the dough. Roll out thin circles from the dough.
9. Cut into strips.
10. Roll a strip around a wooden stick and deep fry the strips rolled on the stick.
11. When brown, remove it from the wooden stick and fill with the prepared peas filling.

GOLD COIN
Serves-5

INGREDIENTS

1/2 cup chopped carrot	1 tbsp cornflour
1/2 cup tinned chopped bamboo shoots	1 tbsp soya bean sauce
1/4 cup chopped beans	1 tbsp vinegar
1/4 cup chopped capsicum	1 tbsp tomato sauce
1/4 cup chopped spring onion	1 tbsp 8 to 8 sauce
1/2 cup boiled mashed potatoes	1/2 tsp sugar
4-5 chopped green chillies	1/2 tsp ajinomoto
10 bread slices	breadcrumbs for coating
oil for deep frying	salt to taste
	pepper to taste

METHOD

1. Boil carrot and beans in 1 cup boiled water in a saucepan for 5 minutes on low flame. Remove from fire. Add finely chopped capsicum and bamboo shoots.
2. Mix with mashed potatoes, cornflour and soya bean sauce, tomato sauce, 8 to 8 sauce, vinegar, sugar, ajinomoto, salt and pepper and mash well with a fork.
3. Cut the hard crust of bread slices with knife.
4. Either leave the slices as square pieces or cut them in round shape with a round biscuit cutter.
5. Press a tablespoon of mixture on round cut slices (or two tablespoons if slices are square).
6. Sprinkle with breadcrumbs (about 1 teaspoon per slice).
7. Deep fry till light brown.
8. Serve hot with chilli sauce.

BROCCOLI FRITTERS

Serves- 4

INGREDIENTS

200 gms Broccoli florets
1   chopped onion
1   tsp red chilli paste
1   egg
3   tbsp flour

1   tbsp cornflour
1/4   tsp ajinomoto
    oil for deep frying
    salt to tase
    pepper to taste

METHOD

1. Remove the stem of broccoli and take the florets.
2. Bring the broccoli florets to boil in 1 cup water till tender. Drain off water.
3. Chop it fine.
4. Make a thick chinese batter by mixing egg, cornflour, flour, chopped onion, red chilli paste, salt, pepper and ajinomoto.
5. Add chopped broccoli to it and mix well.
6. Heat oil on full flame. Lower the flame. Make fritters out of broccoli mixture and saute till light brown.
7. Remove on a butter paper and serve hot with chilli sauce.

POTATO CORN FRIED

Serves - 5

INGREDIENTS

1/2	kg potatoes	1	tsp sugar
6	corncobs	1	tbsp vinegar
1/2	cup semolina (rava)	1	tsp soya bean sauce
2	tbsp chopped coriander leaves	1/2	tsp ajinomoto
1	tbsp green chilli paste	1	tsp lime juice
4	tbsp cornflour		oil for deep drying
			salt to taste

METHOD

1. Remove the corn from the cobs and boil in two cups water in a pressure cooker for ten minutes after the whistle.
2. Dry the water, if any, and add coriander leaves, green chilli paste, sugar and salt to taste. Then add 1/2 teaspoon soya bean sauce, 1/4 teaspoon ajinomoto, 1/2 tablespoon vinegar, 1/2 teaspoon lime juice and mix well. Make small round balls and keep aside.
3. Boil and mash potatoes. Add remaining portions of soya bean sauce, vinegar, lime juice and salt to taste.
4. Make flat tikkis out of potatoes. Fill with the corn balls.
5. Close the potato tikkis with the corn filling inside and shape into round or oval shape.
6. Roll in rava and deep fry them.
7. Prepare the other balls also the same way and drain off on a grease-proof paper. Serve hot with tomato sauce and chilli sauce.

DEEP FRIED CASHEWNUT

Serves - 5

INGREDIENTS

100	gms cashewnuts	1	tsp capsico sauce
1	chopped onion	1	tbsp vinegar
3	tbsp cornflour	1/4	tsp ajinomoto
2	tbsp flour	1/4	tsp mixed spices
3	tbsp breadcrumbs	2	tbsp breadcrumbs for filling
1/4	cup milk	3	tbsp water for flour
1/2	tsp red chilli paste		salt to taste
1	tbsp butter		oil for deep frying
1	tsp soya bean sauce		

METHOD

1. Powder the cashewnuts.
2. Heat butter in a wok and fry onion to transparent stage.
3. Add cornflour and stir for a second.
4. Then add milk, chilli paste, powdered cashewnuts, 3 tablespoons breadcrumbs, salt, vinegar, soya bean sauce, capsico sauce and mixed spices and mix well.
5. Remove from fire, spread on a flat greased container to about 1¹/₂ " thickness and freeze till set.
6. Cut into desired shape or squares.
7. Make thick batter with flour and water and roll the cashewnut squares in flour batter. Re-roll in breadcrumbs and deep fry till golden brown.
8. Serve hot with chilli sauce and tomato sauce.

RED BEANS ON TOAST

Serves - 5

INGREDIENTS

100	gms red beans (rajmah)	1	tsp soya bean sauce
2	chopped onions	5	tbsp tomato sauce
8	bread slices	2	tbsp vinegar
1	tsp garlic paste	1/4	tsp ajinomoto
1	tsp ginger paste	3	tbsp oil
1	tsp dry red chilli paste		oil for deep drying
1	cup milk for bread		salt to taste
2	tbsp cream		

METHOD

1. Wash and soak the beans overnight in four cups water with salt to taste.
2. Cook in the same water in a pressure cooker for 15 minutes after the whistle.
3. Dry the water, if any. Add cream and remove from fire to cool.
4. Heat oil in a wok. Fry chopped onions to transparent stage.
5. Add ginger and garlic paste and fry for a minute.
6. Add red chilli paste and immediately add tomato sauce, soya bean sauce, vinegar and ajinomoto.
7. Add the boiled beans and a little salt, if required.
8. Remove the crust off the bread, soak in milk for a second, squeeze out extra milk between the palms and deep fry the bread for a second.
9. Place the boiled beans filling on toast and serve with chilli sauce and tomato sauce.

FRIED WONTONS IN BATTER

Serves-3

INGREDIENTS

For the batter

2	tbsp cornflour		2	tbsp oil
3	tbsp flour		2	tbsp soya bean sauce
1	egg		2	tbsp vinegar
1/4	tsp baking powder		1/4	tsp ajinomoto
1/2	tsp sugar			oil for deep frying
1	tsp garlic paste			salt to taste
4-5	green chillies			pepper to taste

METHOD

1. Make wonton as shown on page16. Work up to point 6.
2. Make batter by mixing egg, cornflour, flour, baking powder, salt and pepper.
3. Roll the wanton in this batter and deep fry them in a wok. Drain and keep aside.
4. Heat oil in another wok.
5. Fry garlic and chopped green chillies.
6. Add soya bean sauce, vinegar, sugar and ajinomoto to it.
7. Put fried wontons in the above mixture.
8. Saute for a minute and add 1 teaspoon cornflour dissolved in 1 tablespoon water. Stir well and remove from fire.
9. Serve hot.

FRIED BROCCOLI

Serves-4

INGREDIENTS

250	gms broccoli florets cut into thin pieces	2	tbsp soya bean sauce
2-3	tbsp cornflour	1	tbsp vinegar
1/4	tsp baking powder	1/4	tsp ajinomoto
1	tsp dry red chilli paste	1	tbsp tomato sauce
1	tbsp ginger juice		pinch of salt
2-3	tbsp breadcrumbs		oil for deep frying

METHOD

1. Mix above ingredients, except broccoli, well to make into a thick batter. Add little water, if required.
2. Boil broccoli for 2 minutes in 1 cup water. Drain off water.
3. Roll broccoli pieces in prepared batter.
4. Roll in breadcrumbs.
5. Deep fry to golden brown.
6. Serve hot with chilli sauce.

PANEER CORN SALT & PEPPER

Serves-4

INGREDIENTS

1/2	cup corn	1	tbsp chopped parsley leaves
200	gms paneer crumbs	1	tbsp soya bean sauce
1	chopped onion	3	tbsp oil
1/2	tsp chopped ginger	1/4	tsp ajinomoto
1/2	tsp chopped garlic	1	tsp black pepper

METHOD

1. Take 4 corncobs and scrape off with a knife.
2. Remove corn from the cobs.
3. Boil it in 2 cups water without salt for 5 minutes after the whistle in a pressure cooker.
4. Cool it; open the lid and dry water, if any.
5. Make paneer out of 1 litre milk (it should make about 200 gms).
6. Heat oil in a wok. Fry chopped onion for a minute. Add ginger and garlic and mix well.
7. Add paneer crumbs to it along with cool corn.
8. Add salt, pepper, ajinomoto and soya bean sauce to it.
9. Cook till it is lightly roasted. Add 2 tablespoons water and cook for 1 minute.
10. Remove from fire, sprinkle chopped parsley and serve hot.

Note: Small bits or cubes of readymade bean curd (about 200 gms) could be used in place of paneer.

GOLDEN FRIED BEAN CURD

Serves-4

INGREDIENTS

200	gms bean curd	1	tsp 8/8 sauce
2½	tbsp flour	1	tsp ajinomoto
1	tsp soya bean sauce		oil for deep frying
1	tsp vinegar		salt to taste
1	tsp tomato sauce		breadcrumbs for coating
1	tsp chilli sauce		pepper to taste

METHOD

1. Take readymade bean curd, cut into 1/2" to 3/4" cubes.
2. Make thick paste with flour, salt, pepper, chilli sauce, 8/8 sauce, tomato sauce, vinegar, soya sauce and 1 tablespoon milk (1 egg could be substituted for milk and 4½ tablespoons flour added in place of 2½ tablespoons flour).
3. Dip bean curd pieces in this batter.
4. Roll these pieces in breadcrumbs and deep fry to light brown.

ALMOND PUDDING
Serves-4

INGREDIENTS

20	gms gelatine (Rex)	50	gms almond powder
3	cups water	1/2	tsp vanilla essence
1	cup orange juice	3/4	cup sugar
1	cup orange fruit	1	cup cream beaten on ice
1/2	tin condensed milk		

METHOD

1. Dissolve gelatine in 3 cups water and bring to boil.
2. Add sugar and cook till sugar dissolves.
3. Strain and cool.
4. Add orange juice, orange colour and vanilla essence.
5. Peel the orange, remove seeds and the segment skin and take the inner pulp.
6. Add the orange pulp to the gelatine mixture.
7. Add condensed milk.
8. Soak almonds in warm water. Peel the skin, grind and add to the above mixture.
9. Pour into a pudding container and keep in freezer for 1/2 hour, then shift to fridge compartment.
10. Serve chilled with beaten cream.

CHINESE DESSERT

Serves-5

INGREDIENTS

1	tin fruit cocktail (450 gms)		1/4	tsp vanilla essence
3	tbsp gelatine		1/2	cup beaten cream
3	cups water		1/2	tsp lime juice
1/2	cup sugar			

METHOD

1. Dissolve gelatine in water in a heavy bottom pan and cook on fire for 5 minutes till completely dissolved.
2. Add sugar to it and cook till sugar dissolves.
3. Remove from fire; strain and cool completely.
4. Add cream and mix well.
5. Set in the freezer for 1/2 hour till completely set.
6. Cut it with any biscuit cutter to desired shape.
7. Drain off syrup from the fruit cocktail tin.
8. Chill the syrup, add 1/2 tsp lime juice to it.
9. Mix the fruits with the gelatine cubes.*
10. Pour 1/2 cup of the syrup and serve.

---

* Making of gelatine cubes is from (1) to (6) above.